CW00547288

Note;

The Editors would like to draw the readers attention to the fact that articles presented in this book are in some instances the memories of factual events as experienced by individual members over half a century ago. Where possible the editors have added footnote but left undisturbed their original text. While we have consulted Navy records and noted official narratives in the Submarine Museum archives and public record offices, some of the incidents as seen through the eyes of the authors may vary in context from those records (That is not to say that those records are 100% correct); Any corrective errors within fall on the shoulders of the Gatwick Submarine Archive committee.

This publication is presented as a serious work of reference, mainly from the lower deck point of view, which would otherwise remain untold.

As with our first two volumes SUBMARINE MEMORIES and MORE SUBMARINE MEMORIES It is also intended as something of an 'Aunt Sally' to gather in other information, corrections and opinions from ex-submariners.

Our archive is not open to the public but we would be happy to receive letters, or phone calls on 01903 813742.

Clyde Gun's Crew

Gatwick Submarine Archive
HADLEY, Upper Beeding
West Sussex BN44 3TQ

EVEN MORE SUBMARINE MEMORIES

MORE LESSER KNOWN FACTS FROM THE GATWICK SUBMARINE ARCHIVE

NOTE - DEFINITION: SHIP - BOAT
A boat can be hoisted inboard; early submarines were small and could be hence 'Our time in boats'

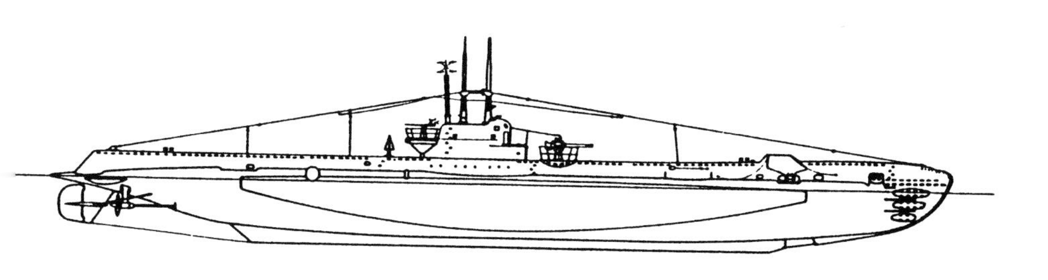

Archive Committee Members

Keith Nethercoate-Bryant
Colin Hunt
Bill Sherrington
Stan Murray

Foreword

By Rear Admiral Dick Heaslip CB
Flag Officer Submarines/ComSubEastLant 1984-87

You can read a number of good histories about submarines, but none of them will tell you what kind of men served in them or how it felt day to day. Gatwick Branch have done a notable service with this series of Submarine Memories - if you weren't there, you can see what they had to cope with and the spirit and sense of humour that kept them going. If you were, it will bring it all back.

Those of us who served in the Cold War especially appreciate the inheriance they left us. Oddly enough (and quite unlike the army) we have never taught any of our eventful history in Training Class.

Perhaps we should just issue these marvellous books instead.

Dick Heaslip

HM/SM Conqueror

INTRODUCTION

The Archive was founded in 1988 to record the Gatwick Branch member's ephemera, anecdotes, photographs and their memories of the Submarine Service in war and peace. Aside from research by crew members descendants tracing their service history and historians after naval incidents, no one can fully appreciate the use to which a collection of material, such as ours, will be put to in the future. These little windows into the past are moments of submarine history frozen in time. It is our duty to preserve as much as we can for future generations. We exchange information with the main Submarine Museum where most researchers visit as the first 'port of call'.

This is the third volume of Submarine Memories from our archive, as with the first two volumes we seem to be haunted by PERSEUS and the John Capes story, this will just not go away. Further intriguing facts and happenings are 'surfacing' all the time.

Was the tale of the sacks of gold and silver true? Was the treasure of the Maltese churches really in the magazine of Perseus?? (See vol. one p.17)

The Greek Prefecture of Kephalonia with the help of Kostas Thoctarides and Rena Giatropoulou (the Greek divers who re-discovered the wreck of Perseus) and the Gatwick archive, have produced a splendid book, illustrated in colour, and have been host's to a visit by those next of kin who were able to travel (see narrative).

In this volume we are attempting to present a complete record of all the crew members of lost 'boats' in the years of the second world war; this was a monumental task taken on by one of our Hon. members Eric Smith. We publish name, rank and submarine in A-Z order. Further information can be obtained by contacting the archive which in some cases holds further details of lost submarines.

Profits from this publication will be distributed to our 'ready use' welfare fund (Help within the hour!) our adopted charity RNBT Pembroke House and the Submarine Memorial fund.

The Archive committee are all ex-submariners.

HM/SM Sportsman 1940's
KN-B Left

Keith Nethercoate-Bryant,
President,
Gatwick Submariners Association.

Dedication

This 3rd volume of memories is dedicated to members of Gatwick Submariners Association who have 'crossed the bar'. Since the last volume was published in 1997. Ron Hart BEM., Stan Jones, Ron Bowen, Robbie Lang, Gordon Bowditch, Dr. Douglas Sinclair.

Acknowledgements

Many Association members and next of kin have given us help in the production of this volume; Our grateful thanks go to all those people and especially the following whose contributions have been vital for the volume.
Com. Jeff Tall OBE. RN Rtd. Director Submarine Museum
George Malcolmson (Curator) Submariners Association Branches, Imperial War Museum, International Submariners Association, David Barlow (Chairman Submariners Association) for extracts from 'In Depth' & Tartan Topics.
Our thanks to Mike Critchley (Maritime Books) for permission to use line drawing from Paul Akerman's Encyclopedia of H.M. Submarines 1901-1955. Jack Casemore and Dennis German for their lengthy Submarine Memories and other contributors too many to properly acknowledge in this list.
We deeply regret that to achieve a proper balance of chapters in this volume we have not been able to present every article given to us; However keep them coming for the next volumes.
K N-B.

Contents

Perseus in her Hayday!
c.1930s

Probably alongside HMS Medway, a Submarine Depot Ship.

Note the awning over the conning tower.

PERSEUS REMEMBERED.

On the 19th and 20th may 2000 forty seven next-of-kin of crew members of submarine H.M.S. Perseus, together with ten invited guests attended memorial unveiling ceremonies on the island of Kefalonia, Greece, followed by a wreath laying ceremony over the boat to honour The memory of the 59 crew and a Greek officer, Commander Nicholas Merlin, who lost their lives when the submarine struck a mine some seven miles off the coast of the island and also to honour those Kefalonians who risked their lives to protect and restore to safety, Stoker John Capes, the sole survivor.
Also present were, the daughter of commander Merlin, Liza Merlin-Vassilatos, Helene Houmar, wife of Captain Houmas OBE, whose boat took Capes off the island to safety, Dohn Katsoulakis, Engineer to Captain Houmas, Helen Cosmetatos who found Capes on the beach and Nikos Vandoros who sheltered Capes on the island and aided his escape.
The ceremonies were organised and put into effect with dignity by the Kefalonian authorities and are deserving of the heartfelt thanks of all who were present.

Representing the Kefalonian authorities were:
The Prefect of Kefalonia - Dionysis Georgatos, The Mayor, Municipality of Eleisos-Pronnoi - Andreas Zapandis, The Chamber of Commerce, Poros - Gerasimos Totolos, Official Organiser for Prefecture - Miriam Innes, Official Organiser for Municipality - Fragiskos Voutsinas, The Bishop of Kefalonia, Officers of the Greek Navy, Divers - Kostas Thoctarides and Rena Giatropoulou.
Representing UK authorities and organisations were:
Commander Chris Reynolds for Flag Officer Submarines - Rear-Admiral Stevens, Rear-Admiral Tony Whetstone - President of the Submariners Association and Submarine Museum Trust, with Mrs. Whetstone, Matthew Lodge - British Embassy, Athens, for Captain John Milnes - R.N. Naval & Air Attaché, Athens with Mrs. Lodge, Colin Hunt - Archives Secretary, Gatwick branch of the Submariners Association and UK Co-ordinator for the ceremonies with Mrs. Hunt, Stan Murray - Gatwick branch of the Submariners Association with Mrs. Murray, Ron Mellor - Secretary, Stafford branch of the Submariners Association with partner, Roger Thompson for next of kin with partner. Also present were John Capes Son & Daughter, Gregory Capes & Julie Knappett (nee Capes).

The ceremonies commenced on Friday 19th May, with a church memorial Service in the village of Mavrata, conducted by the Bishop of Kefalonia, followed by the unveiling in the village of a memorial plaque to the crew of Perseus and Commander Merlin by the Mayor and Commander Reynolds. This was followed by tributes to the crew and to the islanders who assisted and protected John Capes.
A further monument was unveiled at the headland of Sarakinikos, Poros, by the Prefect of Kefalonia and Commander Reynolds, dedicated to the patriotic islanders who put courage before fear to shelter John Capes.
An appropriate passage from Homers "Odyssey" is inscribed on the plaque and reads "all the survivors of the war have reached their homes by now and so put the perils of battle and the sea behind them."

In the evening, at the community arts centre in Poros, a memorial ceremony was held where formal speeches were made and presentations took place. Apart from formal exchanges between authorities and organisations, certificates were presented to many islanders who courageously resisted occupying forces during wartime and assisted John Capes during his enforced stay on the island.

On Saturday morning 20th may, some 100 persons boarded a ferry in Pesada harbour, which sailed to a position over "Perseus" for a wreath laying ceremony. This very moving ceremony was conducted in the traditions of

The Royal Navy by the Bishop of Kefalonia, Commander Reynolds and Rear-Admiral Whetstone, followed by a two minute silence and the playing of the "last post". Roger Thompson read out the names of all crew members, wreaths and flowers were then cast into the sea, together with 60 poppies. So ended, what was, for the next-of-kin, an opportunity to put their loved ones to rest after nearly sixty years of uncertainty, an occasion which will surely stay with us for the rest of our lives.

The people of Kefalonia have our deepest respect and gratitude for an event which was so well organised, for their friendship to this country, for the generosity they showed to all who attended the ceremonies, and for the courage of their island people at a very troubled time in their history.

Colin Hunt. Archives Secretary
Gatwick branch.

Capes Memorial to the Islanders

Postscript (1)

During these ceremonies I was asked if I could "Scotch" these stories about John Capes escape from "Perseus" not being believed and was given sight of an official document dated 1955 which showed clearly that the authorities had satisfied themselves at the time that John Capes' account of his escape from the boat was true.

There was no information forthcoming as to why this information had been withheld for so long or why the next of kin had not been given information about their loved ones, something they had been waiting sixty years to find out.

Bearing in mind the number of boats lost in the Mediterranean, what was so special about "Perseus" that the authorities needed to know? I indicated at the time that this information raised a number of questions which since has given me thought to ask myself:

1. Why would they "need to know" 2. Was the boat on more than a normal patrol? 3. Was there something special on board? 4. What was a Greek Submarine Officer (From Kefalonia) really doing on board? 5. Why (Capes story) would the C.O. go through a minefield twice in 24 hours?

Consider this: An islander approached me to say that he remembered this boat being lost and a story on the island at that time that the British had landed.

In a separate approach to John Capes' daughter by another islander he stated that at the time 10 commandoes landed on the island - well armed and specifically 10!

Is there a mystery about "Perseus"? Maybe, but we shall probably never know.

Postscript (2)

In may 2004 the Gatwick branch granted "honorary membership" to Gerasimos (Makis) Totolos "for his efforts to bring about a memorial tribute to the crew of H.M.Submarine "Perseus" and Greek officer Merlin lost off Kefalonia on December 6th 1941 and for his services to the next of kin of crew members"

Submariners Laying wreaths over site of Perseus

Memorial Plaque to the crew of Perseus

H.M.Submarine AFFRAY

Time and place... 20th January 1948 Sydney Australia. Frank 'Buster' Brown.
Had a run ashore with a couple of mates, ending up in a pub in King's Cross. Downed quite a few tots and got chatty with two male nurses from a local hospital.
We were invited back to their quarters in the hospital when the pub closed and having stocked up with a couple of bottles of gin we carried on boozing. Got 'pie-eyed' and ended up in the grounds of the Hospital.
We woke up next morning bleary eyed with fat heads and headed back to 'Platypus', The Aussie depot ship berthed in Watsons Bay, which AFFRAY was alongside when we went ashore the night before. No sign of Affray, and realised we had overstayed our shore leave. We went on board Platypus and reported to a P.O. who took us before the duty officer. A signal was sent to Affray which was heading out to sea through SYDNEY HEADS for the open sea.
"Have three of your ratings on board", signal back from Affray "Tell them to make their own way home" ! We had seven days leave stopped for missing the boat, but we were not going anywhere anyway. We were kept busy on board Platypus, and the grub was great, also managed to get the odd snifter from kind comrades. Hadn't got a clue how we would get back to the U.K. but skipper of Platypus was very helpful; fixed us up with a berth on an Aussie troopship going to New Guinea on the way to Kure in Japan.
We had a month on the island living in the jungle outside the Aussie army camp, a bit primitive but we survived.
Carried on to Kure where after a short stay left for Hong Kong, felt like being home soon on the move again, believe it was a minesweeper which dropped us off at Singapore; couple of days there and caught malaria. Hospital ship in harbour on way home to the U.K. so was well cared for. Arrived in the U.K. still feeling rough and ended up in Hasler hospital. There for a couple of weeks before my wife was notified that I was back in England.
To recap... Joined ASTUTE February 1946, married June 1946, left for the Far East August 1946. Transferred to Affray March 1947 in Hong Kong, then cruised the Pacific, Japan, Philippines, Indonesia and down to Australia via the Barrier Reef stopping at Townsville then Sydney. All very exciting and enjoyable until we missed the boat, that was when you realised how important it was to have good mates. We certainly needed each other when the Skipper of Platypus gave us the signal from Affray. Apart from the malaria I think we enjoyed our little adventure.

Frank Brown, served in submarines 1944 to 1950.

Frank 'Buster' Brown
HM S/M Affray

Affray 1940's

Goodbye Australia

List of Casualties from HM S/M Affray
Lost in the English Channel 16th April 1951

Surname	Rank	Christian Names
Officers		
Blackburn (DSC)	Lieut	J
Foster	Lieut	D J J
Greenwood	Lieut	J L
Alston	Lieut (E)	J H
Lansberry	Lieut RNVR	R C
Shaw	Lieut (E)	F M
Treleaven	Lieut (E)	J M
Allen	Lieut (E)	O H
Welch	Lieut (E)	A G
Cole-Adams	Lieut (E)	M C
Bilton	Senr Comm Eng	W
Linton	Sub Lieut	William Francis
Preston	Sub Lieut	R J
Strachan	Sub Lieut	J G
Longstaff	Sub Lieut	W A C
North	Sub Lieut	R F
Tugman	Sub Lieut	R T
Rewcastle	Sub Lieut	A G C
Kirkwood	Lieut	W J
Mackenzie	Sub Lieut	C I
Mackenzie-Edwards	Sub Lieut	R P
Frew	Sub Lieut	A A
Howard-Johnston	Sub Lieut	R G
Garwood	Sub Lieut	A R
Nickalls	Sub Lieut	H A
Ratings		
Irven	Tel	A H
Green	L/Smn (TV)	W J
Gostling	Sto	B P
Smith	Sto	J D
Temple	Sto	N
Cardno	Sto	R J
Beddoes	Stwd	D B
Vincent	Stwd	R
Pane	AB	P R
Smith	Cook	F R
Wood	LEM	H J
Leakey	AB	G W
Smith	L/Sto	R B B
Harris	Sto	L E S
Drury	Sto	F
Burberry	A/CPO Sto	A H
Denny	A/Elec	F C
Thirkettle	A/PO Sto	J G
Miller	A/L Sto	J
Curry	Sto	R
Bridges	Sto	O A M
Lewis	Sto	W D
Cooper	PO	J H
Cutter	A/RE	J
Barlow	L/Stwd	J B
Horwell	EM (1)	E
Cook	A/L Smn	G D
Gittins	Tel	H
Parker	ERA 2	G
Bennington	ERA 2	D R
Harkness	PO	W R
Woods	PO Tel	F G
Pearson	A/PO	D H
Whitbread	CPO Sto	R A
Trimby	A/L Sto	V G
Ashley	L/Sto	G T E
Hiles	Sto	R G G
Ramplin	Sto	A
Larter	Sto	G R
Hodges	Sto	J E A
Bartrup	EM (1)	D G
Stewart	AB	A J
Worsfold	A/Ldg Tel	Benjamin J
Lees	ERA 3	N C E
McKenzie	CERA	J L
Taylor	ERA 3	M G E C
Royal Marines		
Andrews	Sgt	T J
Shergold	Cpl	E N
Hooper	Marine	A H G
Jarvis	Marine	D W

EMBASSY OF THE
UNITED STATES OF AMERICA
LONDON
THE NAVAL ATTACHÉ

19 April 1963

Dear Mr. Sherrington:

Your expression of sympathy concerning the tragic loss of the submarine THRESHER together with her gallant crew is very much appreciated.

I am sure that our many friends in Great Britain share this great loss with us, not for the material thing which vanished beneath the sea, but for the hundred and twenty nine dedicated men who gave their lives in the service of their country and of world peace.

Sincerely yours,

R. B. Lynch

R. B. LYNCH
Rear Admiral, U.S. Navy

Mr. W. J. Sherrington
Chairman
Submarine Old Comrades' Association
150 Abbotsbury Road
Morden, Surrey

The Submariner (A Doctor's View)

The tragic loss of the submarine Thresher and 129 men had a special kind of impact on the nation... a special kind of sadness, mixed with universal admiration for the men who choose this type of work. One could not mention the Thresher without observing, in the same breath how utterly final and alone the end is when a ship dies at the bottom of the sea... and what a remarkable specimen of man it must be who accepts such a risk. Most of us might be moved to conclude, too, a tragedy of this kind would have a damaging effect on the morale of the other men in the submarine service and tend to discourage future enlistment. Actually, there is no evidence that this is so. What is it then, which lures men to careers in which they spend so much of their time in cramped quarters, under great psychological stress, with danger lurking all about them?

Bond among them

Togetherness is an overworked term, but in no other branch of our military service is it given such full meaning as in the so called "silent service". In an undersea craft, each man is totally dependent upon the skill of every other man in the crew, not only for top performance but for actual survival. Each knows that his very life depends on the others and because this is so, there is a bond among them that both challenges and comforts them. All of this gives the submariner a special feeling of pride, because he is indeed a member of an elite corps. The risks, then, are an inspiration rather t deterrent. The challenge of masculinity is another factor which attracts men to serve on submarines. It certainly is a test of a man's prowess and power to know he can qualify for this highly selective service.

Emotionally healthy

There is nothing dare devilish about motivations of the man who decides to dedicate his life to the submarine service. He does, indeed, take pride in demonstrating that he is quite a man, but he does not do so to practice a form of foolhardy brinkmanship, to see how close he can get to failure and still snatch victory from the jaws of defeat. On the contrary, the aim of the submarine service is to battle the danger, to minimize the risk, to take every measure to make certain that safety rather than danger, is maintained at all times. Are the men in the submarine service braver than those in other pursuits where the possibility of sudden tragedy is constant? The glib answer would be to say they are. It is more accurate, from a psychological point of view, to say that they are not necessarily braver, but that they are men who have a little more insight into themselves and their capabilities. They know themselves a little better than the next man. This has to be so with men who have a healthy reason to volunteer for a risk. They are generally a cut healthier emotionally than others of the similar age and background because of their willingness to push themselves a little bit farther and not settle for an easier kind of existence. We all have tremendous capabilities but are rarely straining at the upper level of what we can do, these men are. The country can be proud and grateful that so many of its sound, young, eager men care enough about their own stature in life and the welfare of their country to pool their skills and match them collectively against the power of the sea.

Dr. Joyce Brothers.
From 'In Depth' magazine of Submariner's Association

Termike

9th April 1995.

Dear Chairman,

I have read with interest the book "Submarine Memories" which was well presented, but I thought you would like up-dating on the story of U2326 which was named "TERMIKE" and numbered N25 by the Admiralty. I have a small snap taken off the Forth.
I joined her on 22nd September 1945 alongside the "Forth" and her Captain was Lt. Langley-Smith, the former No.1 of "GRAPH" [1].
We had a crew of 14 and bunks for 10, I slept on a camp bed under the bunks, it was a tight squeeze and very damp with condensation.
We did a lot of exercises with destroyers and convoys, and the four escorts were amazed at our underwater speed of 10 knots for such a small craft. .
In December 1945 we had to take her to Libau, Latvia, in company with other larger U-boats and hand them over to the Russians.
For some unknown reason it was decided that U2326 would be towed over by frigate, but the tow broke near Peterhead, so called in there for a couple of hours for repairs while the rest of the boats and escorts carried on.
The tow broke again in the North Sea in very rough weather and we lost our tow-ship and did not meet again till we arrived at Kristensand, Norway, just as the other boats were leaving after they had managed a couple of days ashore.
We followed without a tow a few hours later, after a bath and a meal on the frigate, during which time a party was sent on board the boat to clean it out. The crew of the frigate were a great crowd.
At Libau, the Russians would only allow us ashore in parties of 12 under an armed escort, so it was decided that the escorts with the U-boat crews would leave after three days without any demonstrations on U2326's performances.
The crew of the U2326 changed from our chummy frigate to another one and returned to Lisahally via the Kiel Canal.
At Lisahally, we were engaged in scuttling the remainder of the U-boats. The crew of the U2326 was kept together and we had to prepare another type U-boat for France. Just before we were due to sail, the batteries blew up whilst we were on the jetty being paid, so there were no casualties.
Another one was made ready, U2337 I believe, and sailed to Cherbourg in mid February 1946. We only demonstrated a static dive in the harbour, and left after six days in a French MTB.
This was the U-boat that sank with all hands in the Med. a few months later.
Hope this is of interest to the Branch and I wish you well with the Archives.
I believe I recognise Bill Sherrington on one of your photos and seem to remember him at Dolphin Signal Station [2], Blockhouse Corner in 1944.

E. Ditchburn ex Ldgsig.

[1] "Graph" formerly U570 was captured off Iceland.

[2] Guard outside Sickbay at 'Blockhouse' Signal Station, now long gone.

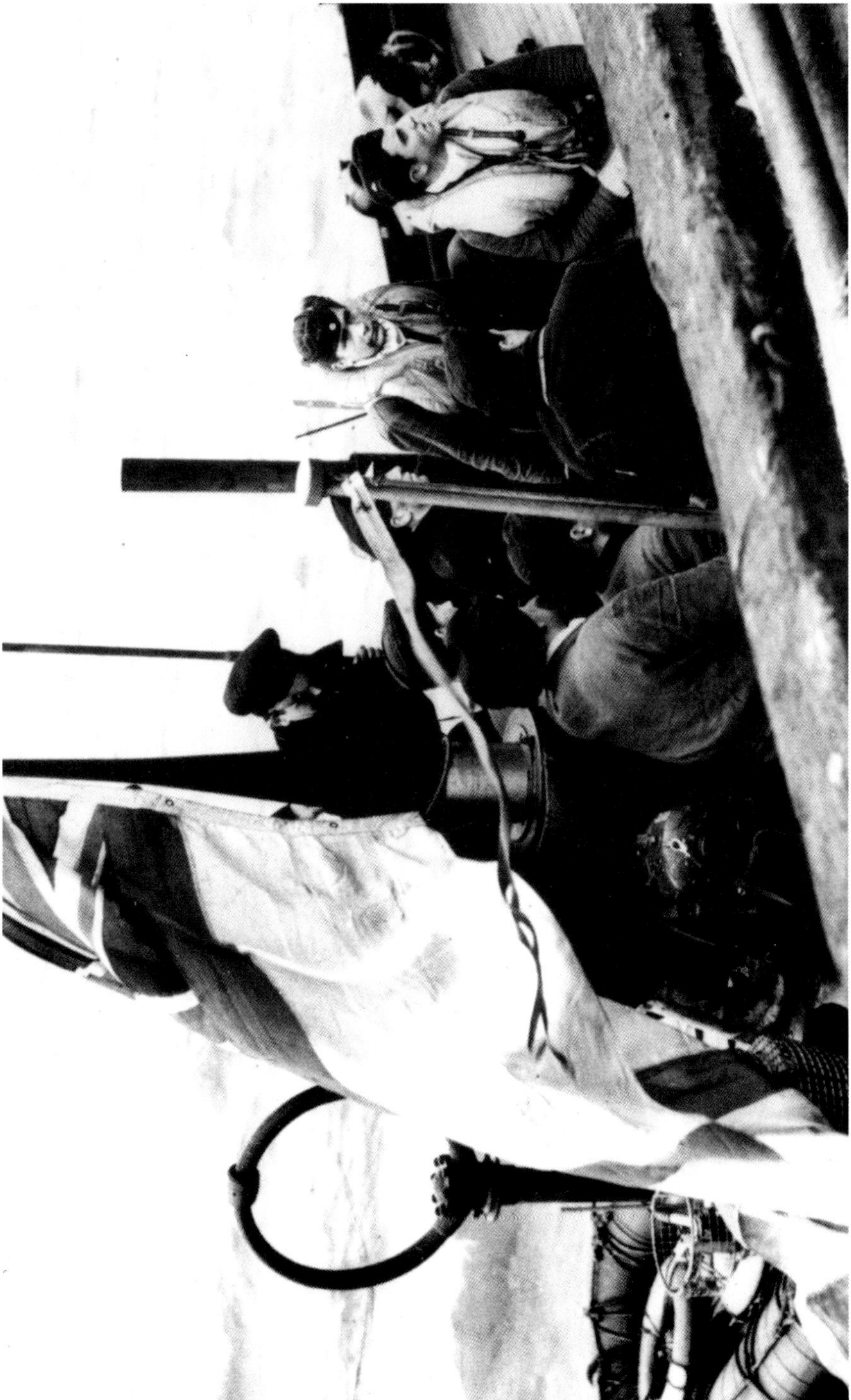

U2326 at Dundee (Under the White Ensign)
Prize crew aboard

R.4 (Above) was the fastest submarine (Submerged) at 15 knots until the advent of the German Type XXI at the end of WWII, which reached 18 Knots underwater in the 1940s.
(HM S/M Scotsman achieved 17 Knots in the 1950s)

‘S’ Class modified conning tower was copied from U1407 ‘Meteorite’

ALBERT GEORGE DAVIES

Lieutenant-Commander Albert George Davies was the last British submariner to sink a Japanese warship in the Second World War.

In April 1945, Davies was commanding the overseas patrol submarine Stubborn on an 11-week voyage from the Clyde to Fremantle to join the Anglo-Dutch 4th Submarine Flotilla, operating under the Americans. He was North of Bali when he heard that a Japanese destroyer was to pass through his area on July 25.

Commencing a day-long watch listening on Asdic with an occasional all-round look by periscope he was "in a funk" lest the Americans deprive him of his first opportunity to fire a shot in action. Nevertheless he managed several hours of good sleep until propellers were heard drawing close. Although the Japanese destroyer Nadakaze was zigzagging wildly, Davies found a firing position. Two in the salvo of four torpedoes fired at 3,000 yards range struck, and his crew's cheers greeted his spontaneous cry of "We've blown his bloody arse right off."

Davies wanted a prisoner for interrogation, but as he manoeuvred amongst the survivors one of them made what was taken as a rude gesture and was promptly shot through the head by the gunnery officer, using his pistol. It was an instinctive and unpremeditated action, but Davies decided that he must shoot all the survivors to prevent reprisals should Stubborn itself later be captured, and he sent for machine-guns to be brought to the bridge without relish.

Looking back years later Davies was convinced that the decision he made was the right one. However, an aircraft forced him to dive and, when he surfaced that night, there was no sign of survivors. In the course of this patrol, Davies also destroyed shipping by gunfire, bombarded a harbour in northern Bali, destroying a jetty and some landing craft, and boarded junks at night; in one of these incidents the gunnery officer went missing.

Davies was awarded the DSC.

Albert George Davies was born on 06 May 1920 at Ramsgate where his household chore was to tear the Daily Mail into 7 squares for the outside privy. Westminster Abbey offered him a choral scholarship, but high Anglicanism over-awed him. Instead he became a contemporary of Edward Heath, the future Prime Minister, at Chatham House School where the fees were four guineas a term.

Encouraged by his father, who had been a telegraphist in the Royal Navy, young Davies sat the Civil Service examination for a naval scholarship, which he passed with good marks to join as a special entry cadet in September 1937.

He recalled that, in his first ship, the light cruiser Newcastle, early in 1939, the official visit of the French President had necessitated for the last time naval officers to wear cocked hats, frock coats, epaulettes and white kid gloves. Soon after the outbreak of war he was at Scapa Flow when Gunther Prien in U-47 sank the battleship Royal Oak. In November he was still in Newcastle when she was adjacent to the armed merchant cruiser I on the Northern Patrol line between Scotland and Greenland. The German battlecruisers Scharnhorst and Gneissenau over-whelmed Rawalpindi, but when Newcastle arrived in answer to an attack signal, the Germans fled under cover of smoke and bad weather, and the intended breakout into the Atlantic was thwarted. The Kriegsmarine's chief of operations coldly noted, "Battleships are supposed to shoot, not lay smokescreens."

Davies career promised well when he was made sub lieutenant of the gun room of the battleship Queen Elizabeth, where he was expected to keep the young Australian, British and Polish midshipmen in order; but after a boisterous evening in Gibraltar, involving a stolen carpet and a runaway car, he was sent in disgrace to the submarine depot ship Medway. Davies's introduction to "the trade" was harder than usual, the bullying "Crap" Miers declaring he would not have Davies in his submarine, Torbay, and E.F. "Bertie" Pizey, captain of Oberon, claiming exclusive use of Davies's childhood name. Being "pot Valiant," Davies told Miers that he wouldn't serve with him anyway, and thereafter he hyphenated his first names, Albert-George.

In August 1941 a shortage of officers meant Davies being lent to the submarine Tetrarch, without the usual training, and his first experience of being depth-charged. Tetrarch had torpedoed an Italian merchant ship in the harbour of Bhengazi, but while withdrawing through the swept channel it ran aground while submerged and was attacked by two destroyers for several hours.

One of the last depth charge salvoes was so close that it blew Tetrarch free of the shingle bottom and it was able to creep away, low on battery power. Davies remembered how swee the fresh air was when it eventually surfaced after dark.

He was navigator of Thrasher in March 1942 when destroyers and aircraft hunted it of Crete. Surfacing afterwards, Davies heard a clanking noise but did not identify the cause After writing up the attack log he went to sleep unaware of what was happening 10ft above him.

Thrasher's captain "Rufus" Mackenzie had decided not to alarm the crew while two unexploded bombs lodged in Thrasher's casing were removed by the first officer, Lieutenan Peter Roberts and the second coxswain, Petty Officer Tom Gould. Roberts and Gould worked regardless of the risk that the bombs might explode when moved and that Thrashe would dive immediately if sighted by the enemy, thus drowning them: they were both awarded the Victoria Cross.

Davies recorded that his own reaction was not to feel lucky that he was alive, but admiration for the enemy pilot's direct hit and empathy for his undoubted chagrin that the bomb had not gone off.

After completing "the Perisher" course for submarine commanders, Davies first comman was the submarine Ursula, where his task was to train a Russian crew and hand it over t the Soviet navy.

From 1947 to 1949, he commanded the submarine Ambush, in which he conducted trial of an improved design of snort mast, which would enable submarines to recharge batterie while remaining submerged. He was then loaned to the Royal Indian Navy as an instructo and studied at the staff college in southern India, and afterwards was first lieutenant of th frigate Sparrow, when she was doubled for Amethyst in making the film Yangtze Inciden

When he retired in 1958, Davies qualified as a barrister at Gray's Inn and worked for som years for the marine insurers Thomas Miler, manages of the UK P & I Club. He was sec retary to the William Hudson shipping company, and latterly worked for the 600 Grou

When Davies realised the unfair anomalies of the Ministry of Defence's pension scheme h crusaded to have them removed through the pages of the Daily Telegraph.

Davies, who died on March 13 2004, married Lorna Hurst, whom he had met during th blitz of Portsmouth. After they divorced in 1964, he married Barbara Hemsley, who died i 1999. Two sons of his first marriage to survive him.

Tartan Topic

H.M.S/m. Tantivy

Built By: Vickers-Armstrongs Ltd. Barrow-in-Furness.
Laid Down: 4 July 1942.
Launched: 6 April 1943.
Pennant Number: P99/P319
Crest: Field: Blue. Badge: A Pegasus courant gold winged white.
Commanding Officers: 24 May 1943 Commander G Rimington, DSC and Bar
19 August 1944: Lieutenant P H May, DSC.

History

October to November 1943: On anti U-boat patrol north west of Stadlandet. Uneventful.
23 February to 22 March 1944: First Far Eastern waters Patrol Sighted a patrol craft in Sunda Strait.
April to 12 May 1944: On patrol west coast Siam and Malacca Strait. On 29th fired torpedoes & damaged ship in Phuket harbour.
On 4th May missed a snap attack on a U-boat. Had another encounter with a U-boat on the 5th. Sunk junk and took prisoners.
to 26 June 1944: On 7 June laid 12 mines off Sembilan Islands. On 19 to 21 June involved in air sea rescue off Port Blair.
4th July to 16th August 1944: On patrol in Malacca Strait. Attacked an escorted M/V.
5th August to 14th September 1944: Diverted to patrol in Sunda trait while on passage to Fremantle. Sunk the escorted 'Shiretoko Maru' of 1800 tons, with 2 torpedo hits, after an earlier attack was foiled by a navigational alteration.
th October to 3rd November 1944: (Lieutenant P H May) 6th patrol in Far Eastern waters. st in south west Pacific area.
On 21st October, 21 schooners were sighted, 8 were sunk by gunfire before aircraft inter-vened. Later, sunk another schooner. Next day a 150 ton coaster and 5 schooners were sunk by gunfire. Attacked by aircraft close to the coast and in shallow water; no damage. Attacked a 500 ton coaster with a faulty torpedo and missed; finished the job on the sur-face with gunfire. Counter attacked by 2 A/S vessels in-effectively, one of which blew up, possibly on the earlier faulty torpedo. On 23rd October, sunk a schooner by gunfire and 2 days later, 2 coasters sunk by gunfire after torpedo failure. On 26th October, 2 more torpe-does failed in an attack on a large coaster; both circling and prematuring. Sunk with gunfire. Left patrol after running 5523 miles, Captain of 8th Submarine Flotilla held Board of Inquiry into unsatisfactory performance of torpedoes.
4th November to 16th December 1944: To patrol east of Singapore; never reached due to various defects and disorders.
4th January to 14th February 1945: On patrol Sunda Strait. Sunk a tug and 2 coasters (in tow). Fired torpedo into Panjang Harbour without result. Went aground very firmly, in what should have been 10 fathom line. There for over 2 hours in view of the enemy, who were apparently unable to take offensive action.

The reason for being in close proximity to the harbour was because U-boats were expected and this was the only place they could go to. The original idea was to get there just before dawn (lucky we didn't). First of all, a fishing stake was mistaken for the first buoy, so we bumped the first time. We then fired the torpedo in what was theoretically the right direction - but no bang. Just as well. Then we turned at rest and went slap into the bank which was incorrectly marked on the chart as 10 fathoms. Finally, the detonators were removed from the heads of the for'ard torpedoes and fired. After jettisoning fuel and fresh water the incoming tide floated the boat off.

19th August 1944 Tantivy Officers (L - R)

Commanding Officer	Lieutenant P. H. May DSC
1st Lieutenant	Lieutenant Kirkwood (Lost on Affray 1951)
Engineer	Lieu-Commander O. St. John
Sub Lieut. Winter	
Navigator	Lieutenant O'Connor
Gunnery Officer	Sub Lieut. Weedon

Note the 'Jolly Roger'

H.M. S/M Tantivy

C/O Lieutenant P. H. May DSC
Skipper of Tantivy

Tantivy entering Portsmouth harbour at end of commission in Far East May 1945

Good Morning 1

The Daily Paper of the Submarine Branch

A PERSONAL MESSAGE FROM REAR ADMIRAL C. B. BARRY, D.S.O.

—ADMIRAL (SUBMARINES)

Office of Admiral (Submarines).

I HAVE pleasure in introducing "Good Morning" a daily paper published specially for the crews of British submarines on operational patrols.

Some well-wishers in Fleet Street are responsible for this unique publication. Sometime ago the Chairman of a well-known newspaper approached the Admiralty with the suggestion that his newspaper should provide a daily magazine-newspaper for our submarines, as some expression of their gratitude for the services of British submarine officers and men in this war. He felt that a novelty of this kind might help considerably to provide topical and interesting reading in spells off duty while on patrol. He suggested that it would be a pleasant and "homely" touch to supply submarine crews with a daily paper which they could open each morning, or whenever their day began—as though they were on shore.

The proposal was approved by the Admiralty, and Admiral Sir Max Horton, the then Admiral (Submarines), agreed that it was an excellent idea. The newspaper company detached experienced members of their editorial staff to produce the paper, with the co-operation of the Office of Admiral (Submarines).

The first number of that daily paper for submarines is now presented, and I take the opportunity of expressing the thanks of the Submarine Service to those who are providing this novel publication, which I am sure will be read with the greatest interest and pleasure in our submarines at sea and aboard submarine depot ships.

I hope all concerned will co-operate in this enterprise by ensuring that the paper is distributed daily in series as numbered, and passed from one to another, so that all will have an opportunity of reading it. I am sure the publishers will appreciate any views or suggestions, or any little personal items of interest which would make it in every way the British Submariners' own paper.

I wish you all good reading—and good luck.

C. B. Barry

Rear Admiral

DOWN THE SLIPWAY

By THE EDITOR

SPEAKING metaphorically, we have bust the bottle squarely over the bows, and "GOOD MORNING," the submariners' own daily paper, is well and truly launched.

There is little doubt that "Good Morning" will "go places" where no other daily paper has gone before, with the most exclusive circle of readers ever served by one publication.

For that reason, it is devised and presented with a one-word objective — entertainment—of a kind which, it is hoped, will shoot a daily shaft of sunlight through the dreariest patrol and the deepest water.

We of the Editorial staff know that, however much you like the contents of "Good Morning" as it is now, you will like them better when you can help us to produce your paper, by telling us what kind of features you favour. More puzzles? More hobbies? More sports features? Scientific articles? Nature and wild life stories? More jokes? More brain teasers? More fiction?

In future issues we have arranged to give you a selection of all these and other items—besides the continuity of the strip cartoons begun to-day.

If you have contributions or ideas, we have the means of putting them in printable form, provided they are not political and do not infringe Service or Security laws, and provided that to all ranks they are—entertainment!

Suppose, therefore, you have any notions for joke-drawings, but cannot draw; send them through to us in the form of the merest scribbles, or just explain them in words, and leave the rest to our artists. If, on the other hand, you are a capable writer, and have something which you think will interest other submariners—send it in, even in pencil.

Particularly we would like to hear from crews who find a way to run their Brains Trust and Puzzlers Contests —and still run a submarine. We have given you something to start on, and we hope to hear how you organise your teams and count up your scores.

Although "Good Morning" comes to you as a daily paper, it is not dated, and its sequence of issue is indicated by the number beside the title on the front page. By a consecutive series of these numbers, the serial nature of strip cartoons, answers to puzzles and such features, may be followed daily.

The address for all your correspondence is: "Good Morning, Press Division, Admiralty, London, S.W.1.

"Bouncy" says: "I'll see yo' getta reply, lads."

First copy of daily paper printed for submarine crews on patrol.

JACK'S STORY

I left school at Easter 1935, when I was fourteen and my mother took me to London to get a job a messenger boy with the Field Press. I earned 14/- per week working from 9am to 6 pm five days a week and some Saturday mornings. I learnt my way all around London, which was to stand me in good stead after the Second World War. After about a year as a messenger boy, I was promoted to office boy and from there was transferred to the editorial side of the Law Times, helping Mr Luscombe the Editor and a lady, I cannot remember her name.

In August 1938, I joined RNVR, putting my age on by one year. I knew there was going to be a war and it was about time the Germans were taught a lesson. At this time, my mother had become ill with a duodenal ulcer and went into Bromley Cottage Hospital for an operation, about mid September. I went to visit her in hospital with my father and sisters, dressed in my new naval uniform; she was rather worried, as she felt a war would soon be upon us. She went into hospital for a second operation and died under the operation; it was very sad for us all.

I had passed my driving test in March or April 1938 and so after my mother had been buried, my lather feeling very sorry for himself, looked to me for company. So he would suggest that we took the car (he had earlier bought a brand new car, a four door Morris 8, cost £128) out for a drive, so we would visit all the pubs in Cudham, Knockholt, Biggin Hill! etc. and I would drive which I liked very much. In June '39 1 did two weeks training as an RNVR on HMS Cumberland a county class cruiser, there was so much bullshit on her and as an ordinary seaman, you were the lowest of the low and the Officers were Gods. I promised myself there and then, that if possible, I would go for small ships where the Officers were more human.

August 1939, 1 was called up and spent three weeks on HMS President, on the Embankment, London. Towards the end of August, 1 was drafted to Chatham Barracks where I was issued with extra kit and had lots of injections for all kinds of illnesses and towards the end of September, I was drafted to HMS Forfar. Formerly she was a Canadian Pacific & Orient liner Montrose but as there was already a destroyer by the name of Montrose, she was renamed. She was 20,000 tons and was very comfortable. The ships company left Chatham by train and it took us 24. hours to get to Glasgow Central Station, we all fell in outside the station and then marched to John Brown's Shipyard at Govan, where the Montrose was in dry-dock being converted into a warship. We had 6"guns forward and 2 aft, I was on A. Gun and it was manufactured in 1908 and the shell was separate from the cordite I had many good shipmates on board, some were Royal Fleet Reserve men and all the young seamen were RNVR's, also RNR men and some were fishermen from Stornaway in the Outer Hebrides. My friends were Joe Oakman, Billy Bragg and Knocker White and a number of others, I cannot remember their names.

When I joined the Cumberland I was put on a table (called a 'mess') where there were 20 or 24 other sailors, the majority of these had left the navy after serving 12 years ? service and were told that if they returned to the navy within 6 months they could re-engage for a further 8 years and then be entitled to draw their pensions having served 21 years ? service. Because there was very high unemployment in the UK in the 1930's, very few

Jack Casemore WWII

people could get any work so they had to rejoin the RN and they all disliked civilians. I, being a civilian, was treated rather harshly.
The first day on board we started work at 6 am., scrubbing the decks with salt water being pumped through a 4" hose, in bare feet and with trousers rolled up to the knees. We were at sea in the North Sea and Atlantic, doing exercises, and as we scrubbed, the smell of freshly baked bread coming up from the galley certainly gave us an appetite. Breakfast was at 7a.m. and 7.30a.m. then it was back to work until 12 noon. Going down to my mess for lunch, the sailors would be getting their "tot" of rum "what do you want down here, stay on the upper deck until the sailors have drunk their rum, then you can come down", I was shouted at. So, I went back to the upper deck and went back down about 15 minutes later. I sat down on a long form at the table, "You are not at home now boy, your mothers not here to wait on you, get up and help dish out the dinner" was the retort this time. Later, after the evening meal had been finished all sorts of activities were taking place. Some men would be making mats, others would be swatting up on the seamanship manual to qualify as a Leading Seaman or a Leading Torpeadoman or a ? ? others were mending their clothes, some were playing cards or writing letters and some were just "skylarking around".
The Leading Seaman of our mess was named Smith and was 35 or 36 years old and a bully; the OD of the mess (the one who had to do all the jobs nobody else wanted to do) was a 28 year old "two badge man" and suddenly L/S Smith would start hitting the OD with a broom, the next thing they would be wrestling, then others would join in and the OD would be held down on the deck and stripped naked. Condensed milk, tomato ketchup, mustard and anything else that would make a mess would be put on his genitals and well rubbed in. He would then be let go and allowed to go and take a shower. The next night they gave me the same treatment, it was one of those things you just had to take in good heart.
A couple of days later, talking quietly to the OD, I suggested that we do the same thing L/S Smith, but he was not keen on the idea. I said I was going to have a go and would he help me. The evening came around and I tormented L/S Smith, who came straight at me. I was beginning to get the better of him when the OD came and gave me a hand and we managed to get him on the deck. We stripped him of his clothes and gave him the same treatment. After showering, he came into the mess and challenged me to a fight; at my face which I ducked and hit him as hard as I could in the solar plexus. His head came forward and I hit him hard on the jaw, he collapsed on the deck unconscious for a few moments and as he tried to get up a number of men also challenged him to a fight. After that I could do nothing wrong and the next day at "tot" time, I was invited down to have "sippers" with a number of men in the mess.
In October, we sailed down the Clyde to Greenock where we did our sea trials and then we started patrolling between Scotland and Iceland, called the Northern Patrol doing CONTRABAND CONTROL and stopped and searched a number of ships. We also had paravones fitted and when we found a mine on the surface, we would have rifle practice and it was surprising how hard it was to hit one of its horns to explode it. We would often see large whales laying on the surface and a number were reported as U Boats, until they blew up a spout of water. We saw many seabirds and marvelled at the gannets diving into the sea and retrieving a large fish or the porpoise that would swim alongside of the ships. Also at night we would see the Aurora Borealis or the Northern Lights as they were more

commonly called. One night, we went to gun action stations and were closed up for a long time with engines at full speed and the whole ship vibrating and the bows leaping out of the water. After some hours closed up, our gunlayer said, "Don't worry lads, the waiting is the worst, once we get into action it will be alright"; he was a RFR man and had been in the Battle of Jutland. Sometime later the ship stopped vibrating, we altered course and went back to patrol routine, it was not until we got back to harbour some weeks later, when we heard that the Rawalpindi, a similar vessel to ours had been sunk by the German battleship DEUTSCHLAND. We were in harbour somewhere early April 1940 and I was bowman of the motor boat and we were cruising round several ships that were at anchor off Greenock, in the Clyde. One of these vessels was a destroyer, the WREN and while waiting for the passenger that had gone in board, I spoke to the boat swains mate at the top of the gang-way and he said that two seamen had not returned from leave and that they were just on their way to Norway, where there was a battle going on. I said I will come with you and I know someone else on Forfar who would like to come. So when we returned to Forfar I was told by the officer of the watch to pack a steaming bag and get over to the Wren. It was Knocker White, a well spoken London lad that came with me and we spent about five weeks in Norway, in Norwegian waters whilst I was on HMS Wren.

My memory is not very clear at this point in time; I was part of ammunition supply to the 4" guns so when we went into action, I was down below and did not see anything. We landed French soldiers in Norway somewhere near Tronesheim and I remember seeing HMS WARSPITE; what a wonderful sight she was and I remember engaging three German destroyers, much bigger than we were. They were modem 2,500 ton ships, we were 1st World War and 900 tons and we had to run for it. We were also attacked a number of times by aircraft, some of which were the dreaded Junkers 87 dive bombers and another time when we were engaged by the enemy, we had part of our bridge blown away. We had to retire and returned to Scotland for repair at Rosyth and then down to France for the evacuation of Dunkirk. Those poor devils were in a state, the majority of soldiers were so demoralised and the terrible stories some of them had to tell, also terrible injuries some of those soldiers had. We had been to Dunkirk three times to pick up soldiers and on the fourth run out from Harwich, was attacked by aircraft. I heard bombs coming down and the next thing I remember is being in the water and a lot of men were also around me. I managed to get to the early float and it was four hours before we were picked up, although the sea was calm it was still quite cold.

We were taken to Chatham Barracks and kited out and sent on survivors leave 14 days from what I remember there were about 50 survivors. One of the complaints by the soldiers we picked up at Dunkirk was, the complete absence of the RAF.

Shortly after returning to Chatham Barracks, I was sent to St Vincent at Gosport, to pass for a torpedo and electrical course, so that I now was a seaman torpedo man. On finishing the course, I was returned to Chatham and suddenly my kit from Forfar turned up, as it had been sent back to Chatham. Kicking about in Chatham Barracks became very boring and my friends and me were getting fed up, when a notice was put up that volunteers for submarines were wanted, 4/- per day hard-layers, so we went along the drafting office and put our names down. Still nothing happened and we were really cheesed off, when the buz went round that a draught was going to Canada to pick up some of the 50 destroyers

America had given us. So we called into the drafting office but were told that as we had already volunteered for submarines, we were not eligible. One of our gang had a friend in the drafting office, so we asked him if we could bribe our way onto this draft. It was a long time ago, but if my memory is correct, it cost each of us £2 to get on to this draft, which left from Liverpool. It was quite a big liner and there were a lot of RAF personnel on board, going over to Canada to train as bomber crews. We were in convoy to start with but half way across the Atlantic. We left the convoy and steamed at full speed to Halifax, Nova Scotia. The destroyer I went to was named by the RN, HMS SHERWOOD a four funnelled top heavy bastard at sea. I think we stayed in Halifax about three weeks. When we first took over these destroyers, lots of cars would pull up by the jetty and invite us to their houses and many of the cars had on their back windows, THERE WILL ALWAYS BE AN ENGLAND, what a morale booster that was. Whilst in Halifax, I met a French Canadian girl who lived with her sister, whose husband had gone to England with the Nova Scotia Regiment. I will not go into detail but I think I learnt a lot from her. Out on the town one day with her, a Canadian family I had met a week or so before, bumped into us, we introduced one another and everybody was conversing. One man came to the back of me and whispered "Do you know she is French." I did not understand the implication at the time.

On leaving Halifax, we made our way to St Johns, Newfoundland. There was six feet of snow in the city and was told 12 feet outside of the city. We had a wonderful reception there and the main meeting place was the ice rink, all the local beauties went skating and my run ashore oppo and I met two beauties. My girl's father was the manager of the big paper mills and offered me a job, if I thought of deserting. He did not think I had much of a future if I went back to England, however, some days later we cast off for the UK. I think it was about the fourth day at sea, I woke up this morning feeling particularly cold and the ship was rolling like a bastard. My job on board was an electrician's mate, so I was on day work. The seamen had rigged up a lifeline, running aft of the bridge to the superstructure, going down to the engine room. It was some time in the forenoon and I have never seen seas like these, waves 50 ft high towering above us, then crashing down on us and submerging us for what seemed like minutes at a time. The only way anyone could get aft along the lifeline was as soon as the ship came to the surface, run like hell along the lifeline, hoping you reach the after superstructure before the next wave came over. Some stokers aft in the engine room, had got injured and the sick-bay Tiffy (we did not carry a doctor) was going aft to attend them. As he ran along the lifeline, a hawser real broke adrift and crashed him against the starboard tubes, cutting both his legs off about 9" above his knees but one leg was hanging by the sinews. When that wave had gone and we broke surface, we saw him jammed on the tubes, myself and another seaman went to rescue him and pulled him to the lifeline. Holding one of his hands and my other hand holding tight to the lifeline, the next wave crashed over us and suddenly the other seaman let go. I last saw him on the top of the next wave coming at us. By this time another came to my rescue and we managed to get him forward into the sick-bay, where we saw the extent of the damage to the sick-bay Tiffy's legs He was fully conscious and told me to cut his trousers away and told me that the sinews had to be cut, to take his leg off his other leg was already completely off. I think there were about five sinews, he told me where to find the scissors

and I tried to cut one through, he screamed like hell but when I stopped he said "You have got to cut them through", so I carried on and I think I managed to cut through two of them, when the coxswain and a lieutenant came to our rescue and took over from me and the seaman, I remember standing on the leaside of the forward superstructure and being as sick as a dog.
Shortly after this had happened, an electric motor broke down underneath the boiler room, in the bilge's and the commissioned torpedo gunner and myself went down to get it working again. (Petty Officer torpedo gunner's mate and a leading torpedo man, were repairing something else). As I remember we were down there several hours and I received a very good report from the officer.
Appendix:
I ran over to him and pulled him to the lifeline, another man came to help me hold him on the lifeline as the next wave came crashing over us but unfortunately this n was not holding the lifeline hard enough and he was washed over the e; the last I saw of him was on of a wave towering above me but a little aft. Another sailor came to our help and eventually we managed to get this legless man into the sick-bay. On cutting away his trousers, we could see one leg had been very neatly amputated but his other leg was hanging on by a number of sinews. The injured sick-bay attendant was fully conscious and told us that his leg had to come off and that I had to cut these sinews and pointed to a drawer or cupboard where kept his scissors. Every time I tried to cut through these sinews, he would scream with but when I stopped, he insisted that I carry on. As far as I can remember, I had cut through two sinews when a Petty Officer an Lieutenant came into the sick-bay and I explained what had happened and what I was trying to do, they said "all right, we will take over now" and with that I went out onto the leaside of the upperdeck sheltering under the superstructure and was seasick.
It took us seven more days to sight land and landed our sick-bay Tiffy in Belfast. I spoke to him as he went ashore on a stretcher but I noticed he had quite a smell, I hope it was no gangrene, he was a very brave man. This was towards the end of November or December 1940. We then proceeded down the Irish Sea to Portsmouth where we went into dry-dock for repairs; shortly after this I was drafted into submarines. I did my submarine training course, which I think lasted three weeks, the best part was the diving tank which was escaping from a dummy escape chamber, in a submarine and then I went into spare crew in Pactolus shed.
HMS Unbeaten had just come in from her first patrol and was getting ready to go out to the middle east, probably Malta; all of the crew were given seven days leave and on their return, one seaman had gone sick. I had become chummy with the crew and volunteered to take his place, so in one one two, I was a member of Unbeaten's swashbuckling crew preparing to go out to the Middle East. We had a last run ashore with some of the crew and had gone on the ferry to Portsmouth. We were in a pub at the top of Queen Street, when an air raid started, it was not until the bombs started dropping that we evacuated the pub and sheltered under Woolworth. the bombs were coming close so we decided to run over to Aggy Westerns and a bomb hit Woolworth's just where we were standing. We began to get the wind up as it seemed they were targeting us. Someone said they knew where there was an air raid shelter, so we crossed the road again and started to go towards the harbour, when

Aggy Westerns was hit. Arriving at the air raid shelter, we found the police there as it had received a direct hit and was told the next day that 500 people had died in that shelter, the night before. The next day I was in the back of a RN 3 ton lorry, for what reason I cannot remember and on passing the Town Hall, there were flames still coming out of the roof. Shortly after that Unbeaten sailed for Gibraltar, we did a seventeen day running patrol down through the Bay of Biscay and on surfacing in sight of Gibraltar, in brilliant sunshine, I had my first view of the Rock, a sight I will always remember.

We tied up to the Maidstone, the 8th Flotilla parent ship and stayed there about one week, Dicky Dowdell L/Stoker Sturman and myself had a run ashore. We went around the different bars, drinking green and purple and yellow liqueurs and we were hopelessly drunk, so we decided to go to La Linea, across the border in Spain. There was a big green span between Gibraltar and the British border control, manned by British soldiers. We told them where we wanted to go but they very politely told us we were not allowed over the border, so we staggered back to Gibraltar, up through Alameda Gardens and back to Maidstone; some days later we sailed for Malta. We had an uneventful patrol to Malta but on our second or third patrol we went to gun action stations, with a schooner off the North African coast, which I found very exciting, as I was guns crew; our gun was a 12 pounder. First of all I would like to explain our procedure in surfacing for gun action. Our captain would get fairly close to the target, then go down to 60ft, when everyone was ready, hydro planes hard to dive blow main ballast tanks, open conning tower hatch at 40ft. Three of the gun crew would be in the tower and the rest on the ladder, in the control room. The water would pour in and the first time I did this, I thought it was the end but suddenly we were being sucked out of the boat and all of the water as well, onto the bridge, over and climb down the outside of the conning tower, off clips and train the gun, undo the shell locker and load the gun. Other shells would be passed up the conning tower and we would fire into the hull of the wooden schooner. these schooners would be carrying supplies for the German or Italian army and I remember seeing the native crew running along the bowsprite and diving into the sea. A few days later, we sighted a ship about 5,000 tons, off Tripoli and went into attack it, this was on the 19th May 1941 and my sister Joan was married on the 20th May. This is one reason that I remember, also this was the first time I had been depth charged. On sighting the target we were summoned to diving stations, my job was the helmsman and after carrying out the attack and getting into the best position, we fired three torpedoes, very shortly after there was aloud explosion and we broke surface. Then we started to be depth charged, all of the lights went out and reports from different parts of the boat were reported to the control room. Water flooding from the stern glands, forward and after escape hatches leaking, smell of battery gas reported. We hit the bottom, whether a depth charge on top of us pushed us down, I do not know but whilst all this was going on and our 1st Lt. was stuttering out his orders of pump forward or pump aft. I suddenly wanted to pay a penny, so I asked the 1st Lieut., he told me to use the officer's heads, this I did but he put his heard round the door and said in a loud whisper, "do it on the side, you are making HE", this goes to show how tense everyone is when being depthcharged.

After a very long time of altering courses and the destroyer above dropping more charges, our Captain decided to lay on the bottom, if possible, so we drifted slowly down and laid on the sea bed. The duty watch took over and the rest were told to turn in and go to sleep

but do not make any noise; eventually we heard the destroyer run over the top of us and disappear into the distance. We waited two more hours to make sure he had gone, then very gently ran our pumps to lighten our ballast tanks, so that we could surface. this took some time, as I think we could have been stuck in the mud but eventually we broke free and ran slowly away for about half an hour, then surfaced. After a while we started our main engines and got the hell out of our last position. We shortly after that returned to Malta, our patrols from Malta lasted between 17 and 21 days and our time in Lazareto Base was about 7 days, so we were doing about one patrol a month and nearly every patrol something happened. We would either sink something or attack something and miss or damage a ship and often get depth charged, when the Upholder sank two 20,000 ton troop ships, we were in the area with her and I will tell you the Unbeaten's version of what happened to us.
Almost all the 10th flotilla submarines covered an area between Sicily and Tripoli, to name some of them being Upholder, Urge, Unbeaten, Utmost, Upright and Ursula. Unbeaten sighted the convoy of four 20,000 ton troop ships and we sent out messages to the other submarines; we had difficulty in getting to a position where we could attack but at last fired four torpedoes. Almost immediately, first one troop ship was hit, which sank and then the following troopship was hit, it was not our torpedoes, as our torpedoes were still running and could not have reached their target in that time. This was a night attack on the surface and we dived and steamed away from the target and closed all watertight doors for depth charging. Nothing happened, up periscope and the captain exclaimed "My god, everything is lit up, search lights everywhere", so we surfaced and started to re-load our torpedoes and charge our batteries. As soon as we had re-loaded, this took several hours as our mess and all the stores and hammocks and bedding had to be moved into the passage way to enable us to re-load and this was in the height of Summer and there was no such thing as air conditioning in those days. Having re-loaded our torpedoes we returned to the scene, one troopship was still afloat, with destroyers still picking up survivors. We started our attack on the damaged ship and was about to fire when she blew up, one minute later our asdic rating Jock Burnie, reported fast running H.E. sounds, like a torpedo. We immediately flooded Q and went to 90ft and she passed right over the top of us, some short while after we heard the strangest noise as though there were nets being pulled over us. It was only later, when our captain said all trace of the troopship had vanished but the destroyers were still picking up survivors, that I realised the noise we heard was the troopship breaking up as she went down. What had happened was, the Upholder, who was on the next billet to us had fired two torpedoes at the first troopship and two at the second one, hitting the first and sinking her and damaging the second. When she had re-loaded she went under the damaged troopship and sunk her from the other side and the torpedo we heard coming straight at us was one of hers; David Wanklin was awarded the VC for this action. The Swordfish of the Fleet Air Arm from Malta, sank the third troopship and the fourth troopship was sunk in Tripoli harbour by Wellingtons of the R.A.F.
One of the most emotional things that happened to me one day in the summer of 1941, July or August, was on returning to Lazoreto Base after a rather trying patrol. We had been in harbour for about two days and had heard that Union was overdue and had been sunk. Some of our crew were detailed to empty the lockers of the seamen and stokers of Union and stow each individual's items in their kitbags so that a new boat coming from England

and stow each individual's items in their kitbags so that a new boat coming from England could use their lockers.
About four of us from Unbeaten were given the job and on cutting the locks off started to put their belongings into their kitbags. On opening the lockers we were confronted with photographs and letters from their wives, girlfriends and mothers as well as their personal clothing and mementos that these friends of ours had in their lockers; one could not help reading some of the letters and wondered how this poor bastard had died. Would we on the Unbeaten very soon face the same fate and would some other submariner then be stowing my personal things in my kitbag?
We did three gun actions against schooners along the North African Coast and one against a railway bridge on the East Coast of Italy. We had taken on board in Malta, three or four soldiers who were going ashore in Italy to blow up a bridge. We landed them by a canvass boat that they rowed ashore on a moonless night to lay charges under a railway bridge, which was possibly guarded by Italian troops, so that when a train went over the bridge the charges would blow up; they laid their charges under the bridge and returned to Unbeaten before daylight.
I think it was about 11a.m. when at periscope depth we watched a train approach, on arriving at the bridge it was halfway over when it blew up, derailing the train but the train was still on the bridge. Soldiers could be seen around the train, so Unbeaten surfaced and went to gun action on the train; after giving a number of hits on the train aircraft was spotted and we had to dive.
Our 2nd Coxswain sewed a train on a bridge on our skull and crossbones flag.
Jock Bernie joined Unbeaten in the summer of 1941 in Malta. I think he had been on the UPRIGHT before he came to us and I believe he was a survivor of the Unity which was rescued by one of our own convoys in the North Sea. He was short, scruffy and had hair and a beard which was grey to fair and his beard stuck out at right angles to his face; but on his asdic set he was faultless. On being attacked he would give a running commentary on what the destroyers were doing even telling when the depth charges had hit the water intermingled with lots of funny comments that helped to ease the tension in the boat. He was also a very good caricature artist and if something out of the ordinary happened in the course of a day, that night a cartoon would go up on the notice board. For example, one day in the summer of 1941 suddenly "Captain in the Control Room" was called. Teddy Woodward jumped from his bunk, he was in the nude but wrapped a towel around himself and started the attack. Half way into the attack the towel fell from him, but he carried on the attack naked. That evening Jock's cartoon went up on the notice board with the caricature of Teddy dancing round the periscope with the biggest genitals imaginable. We all thought that Jock had gone too far and that he would get a telling off by the skipper, but so Teddy loved it and I believe he kept all the cartoons that Jock did.
During the late autumn or winter of 1941 a young telegraphist, named Hadden, joined our boat and one day on patrol, we came off watch together and were standing in the galley drinking a cup of cocoa when there was a scraping noise on the outside of the pressure hull. Hadden said to me in a rather strained voice, "what is that"? I replied rather nonchalantly, "Oh I expect we are running through a minefield, don't worry we are below them, this sometimes happens, its nothing to worry about. Wasn't I naïve?

During the later half of the Summer, into the Winter, our patrols continued sinking merchant ships whenever we intercepted them. One incident I remember, on attacking a target, which I think we missed, due to our torpedoes porpoising and was then attacked by two destroyers who repeatedly depth charged us. We took evasive action but could not shake them off and went deeper because the depth charges were so close. Eventually, getting to 220ft but then found we could not maintain our depth and was going still deeper, we could only run our pumps to pump water from our tanks when depth charges were dropped, otherwise the destroyers above would pick up our pumps running and give our precise position away. We were gradually going deeper, our maximum safe diving depth was 250ft, then red for danger for the next 100ft, then there were no markings after that. We went down to 350ft and the pressure increased outside, it was estimated that we went to more than 400ft when our captain decided that at the next lot of depth charging, he would blow our main ballast to enable us to come up to about 220ft, this he did and as the echo of the depth charges faded, we started slowly to move upwards; at 250ft, we were rising much too fast and could not stop her and shot to the surface. By this time we had flooded our tanks to try to stop us breaking surface and immediately went racing to the bottom again, hitting the bottom at about 220ft, we stopped our main motors and everybody was told quietly not to move, as the sea bed should have been much deeper than this and we might be laying on the side of a hill. After a short time, our captain said except for the coxn on the after planes and the Chief Tiffy (the engineer) and himself, everybody should lay down where they were and close their eyes. We heard the destroyers go over us a couple of times, then after several hours, we heard their H.E. fade into the distance. Some hours later, as we had not heard the return of the destroyers, we decided to see if we could get off the bottom. We very quietly blew one and six main ballast tanks but nothing happened, after a short while, we blew them a little more robustly and after a pause we felt the boat move, so grouped down, we slowly started our main motors and then saw our depth gauge needle move and very slowly slid to the surface. On opening the conning tower hatch, the inside of the boat was filled with thick fog and the fresh air smelt terrible but this soon cleared when our main engines were started and the destroyers were nowhere to be seen. It was very dark as the moon had not yet risen, we all felt God had been on our side that night.

In harbour at Lazareto Base, Sleima, Malta, the bombing gradually increased and one day our mess got a direct hit and although we had not noticed it before, .there were two arches on opposite walls and these had been blown in. There was a small room which had been bricked up at some much earlier date, inside this small room were sea chests with letters from captains. The sea chest that I commandeered was full of letters somewhere between 1 850 to about 1 880, the letters were in beautiful hand writing and told where they had come from and what they were carrying as their cargo and what their destination was and lots of them had 1 penny blacks and 2 penny blues. When I was much younger, I had saved stamps so knew a little about them and thought they were worth keeping, so I put some of them into my kit bag, nearly a quarter filling it. Over the next few years, I gradually lost some of them and after the war was over I gave them to my nephew, young Arnie.

Carrying on with my story of our patrols on Unbeaten; the pattern of patrols was similar but different locations; sometimes we would be patrolling round Italy or Sicily or the North African coast, where ever the targets were, we would receive these from Rugby. I think this

was 8pm or 8am and it was rumoured that we had spies in Italy, somewhere between the 1
5th and 20th December '41, we had information that the Italian fleet were going to leave Taranto, so our flotilla was urgently sent there, all spread out to intercept this battle fleet. In the late evening, we heard very faint H.E. in the distance, we were on the surface, charging our batteries hoping that we were the ones to have a go first at this massive battle fleet and so it was, as this fleet got nearer the noise was quite terrifying. Firstly, we had to dive under some E boats, surfaced shortly afterwards and then we heard and saw the bow waves of destroyers. All four torpedoes were ready to fire as this large battle fleet came into our line of fire, when suddenly they altered course and came straight for us and I can still see their massive bow waves coming straight for us. We crash dived to 90ft and heard the roar as they went straight over us, everyone was so disappointed but also relieved. We sent a signal to Urge and Upholder, the position of the Italian battle fleet but shortly after they returned to Taranto. All of the 10th SM flotilla returned to Malta and had Christmas at Lazareto Base, unfortunately I got into a fight over our Christmas dinner and had two bottom teeth knocked out.

Leading Stoker Sturman was a personal friend of mine as well as a member of our crew on Unbeaten and a run ashore oppo. In about September 1941 Sturman, Dickie Dowdell and me had a run ashore to Valletta or Sleima; the night before Sturman said that he had been uffering from some very bad headaches and we had said to him "go to see the quack". The ollowing morning Sturman went to the sick bay; on seeing the surgeon , a Lt. Commander, he asked him what boat was he from, when Sturman replied the Unbeaten, the quack eplied "you are going on patrol the day after tomorrow aren't you" and Sturman said yes I hink so. The quack said "yes I know your trouble, get back down the boat and lay off the eer". When we asked Sturman how he had got on he said "I would rather die first than ave to see him again"

About one week later, whilst on patrol, Sturman was found dead in the fore ends. I emember helping Jock Forbes, our 2nd Coxswain, to tie heavy spanners from the engine oom to his legs and body with cod line and then to sew his body into his hammock and ash it up. That night we took his body onto the casing; the Captain said a short prayer and turman was lowered into the sea

Our next patrol was around Sicily and one day, just after daybreak, we were already dived, hen suddenly the officer of the watch suddenly saw a submarine and quickly summoned he captain into the control room. We started the attack straight away and within 15 inutes had sunk U 375, a German U Boat, hitting her I believe, with 3 fish (torpedoes). s we proceeded to go through the debris some few minutes later, we suddenly saw some-ne try to grab the periscope, our captain quickly looked around for aircraft, then surfaced nd we picked up one survivor (what a lucky man). We dropped him down the conning wer and on landing in the control room, proceeded to be sick and spewed his stomach up ith plenty of spaghetti. As the captain came down into the control room, our German U oat man, stood to attention and said," Hr Captain, Geneva Conventions, I claim my rights a prisoner of war", (this was said in German, but we understood what he meant). We had out two more weeks to do on patrol, so he slept in the P.O's Mess but would come into e fore-ends to talk to us seamen and stokers and one day, one of our crew said to Hans och, that was his name. "Old Jan Hitler is a brown hatter", on explaining what that was,

Hans looked quite angry and said in a loud voice, "Churchill brown hatter" and we all roared with laughter. On seeing it was our sense of humour, he joined in the laughter. During this patrol, we sighted a convey and confirmed it was Italian, my job was to guard Hans in the P.O's Mess and was given a revolver to do this. On being told we were chasing an Italian ship, he was quite adamant, "sink the bastards, Italians no good". He also asked us about our depth gauge and when it was pointed out to him there was three feet to his metre and our maximum diving depth was 250 feet, he laughed boastfully and said, "German U Boats can go down 300 metres, that is how we get through Gibraltar". This information was later got from him when we put him ashore in Lazareto Base, Malta and he was put in a cell where the coxn of the Polish submarine, SOKOL had been put as he spoke fluent German and was told to make out he was a merchant seaman and had been sunk nine months before; all this came out whilst they talked to one another. Another little episode, whilst talking about Hans Ploch; I was casing party on Unbeaten (that is on entering or leaving harbour I was on the upper deck) and as he was going ashore into the base. Captain submarines of our flotilla was leaning over the balcony of the wardroom o Lazareto Base and I shook hands with our prisoner and wished him luck, when Captai S/M shouted as loud as he could, "Put that man in my report for fraternising with th enemy," but I heard nothing more about the incident.

On our next patrol, Unbeaten sunk another U Boat, an Italian one this time and she was a big one, but there were no survivors and we could not surface to make sure as there wer several aircraft in the area. Sometime about this time, I decided to get ashore before th bombing started, it was generally just after 10am and then again at 3pm in the afternoon Dickie Dowdell, my run ashore opo was coming with me but changed his mind at the las moment. Well, I set out on my own, there was some waste ground between the base and th little bridge on the SLEIMA front, the air raid sirens had already gone but I thought I coul get ashore before they arrived. Well I was halfway across this waste ground when th bombs started to fall, I believe they were dive bombers and they were targeting our bas and submarines and as they were pulling out of their dive, they were machine gunning; firs the bullets were in front of me and then they were just behind me. I was so petrified, I wa running backwards and forwards and eventually hid under a hugh oil tank of severa 100,000 gallons of diesel. After the raid was over, I walked back to the base, it was in a he of a state; I would like to emphasise the terrific noise of the aircraft, the bullets and the ant aircraft guns, at that moment in time. The discipline at the submarine base, at this time, wa virtually non existent; we were going ashore in seaboots and our working clothes almos We were expecting to be invaded anytime and were told, when ashore if we heard there ha been a landing, to get back to the boat as fast as possible because our orders, if th happened, were to get to sea as quickly as we could.

Sleima was in a hell of a state, buildings were laying in rubble and very few bars were ope When we came in off patrol, we would only work down the boat till 12 o'clock midday, th duty watch would have a make and mend and the non duty watches could go ashore, to g away from the bombing. I would catch a bus to Musta, a town near th centre of Malta and walk up to Mdina or St Paul's Bay. On the outskirts of St Paul's, I use a cafe to have a drink and if they had any food, have something to eat, generally a bit o bread and cheese and would chat to a girl that served in the bar. One day, the owner, wh

Lazzaretto Submarine Base, Malta.

(1941 – 1944)

Home of the Unforgettable 10th. Submarine Flotilla

This is the photo of Unbeaten after the refit at Chatham Dockyard. We had the bows cut off level and then rebuilt after being blown to the surface in Malta where the bows were bent 15 degrees out of true as were the Torpedo tubes. Probably Sept. Oct. 1942. The two external tubes were not replaced.

was the girl's uncle, asked me, "do you like Madalene", that was the girl's name. I replied, "yes, she is very nice". He said, "You see she is pregnant, her boyfriend was a pilot in the RAF and he has been shot down, would you like to marry her to give the baby a name, I will give you £100 and a flat to live in, if you say yes". I was very tempted, as I had a premonition that I was not going to survive much longer, I even wrote to my sister Joan, telling her what I might do but I said not.
By this time, Shrimp Simpson, our flotilla Captain S/M, decided that submarines tied up along side or on the trot, were too easy a target for the Luftwaffe, as P36 was sunk in Lazareto Base and another badly damaged; so when we returned to Malta from our next patrol, we entered Merseda Creek at night, unloaded torpedoes and what stores we could and at 6am the next morning, a skeleton crew took the Unbeaten round to Sleima Creek and in the centre of the creek, between Teeni Point and Manoel Island, we dived and laid on the bottom at 50 feet, well out of the way of the Luftwaffe. Lt. Place, V.C our 1 St Lt, who joined us in December or January, was in charge, our POT, an ERA, a stoker and two seamen, I being one of them, the other was Duggy Upton. As soon as we had stopped our motors and gently hit the bottom, we had breakfast, tidied the boat, then turned in for a well deserved sleep. I was in my hammock, in the fore- ends, with Duggy Upton and a stoker, I remember somewhere after 10 am we heard bombs exploding but was not worried, they could not see us, we were in 50 foot of water, so went back to sleep. Suddenly we heard a bomb coming down, we all sat up in our hammocks, I looked at the clock, it was 10.40 am and this bomb got louder and louder and time dragged on. It seemed ages before suddenly, red white, yellow, blue and green lights flashed through the boat, the next I remember is finding myself in the corner of the after port bulkhead, with my two boatmates. We could hear water pouring into the tubespace but the bulkhead doors were closed and we had water leaking from the forehatch, also, all the lights had gone out, so we were in complete darkness. Scrambling to our feet and trying to think what we should do, I said to our stoker, "do you know where the flood valve for this compartment is." "Yes, he said, "O.K this is your job" and the other chap said "we will need to lower the twill trunk". I said "that will be your job". I then checked through to the compartment immediately aft of the fore- ends, which was the accommodation compartment. On shouting through the voice pipe, as loud as I could, suddenly a voice answered, it was Lt. Place an they were O.K in the after compartments, so the bulkhead door was opened and we went into the control room. We reported that we heard water pouring into the tube space and the forehatch was tightened to stop that water and we waited until Capt. S/M came over in a rowing boat and rang a bell under the water to tell us to surface but we were bow heavy. After consulting with the ERA, it was decided to pump air into the tube space to see if that would dispel the water, after doing this and trying to surface several times, eventually the boat moved and blowing our tanks more we finally surfaced; later we were told by the anti aircraft guns crew that we were blown to the surface upside down. On examining the fore- ends compartment on the starboard side, near where my hammock was strung, the pressure hull was bent into the ribs.
Shortly after this incident, we went round to Grand Harbour and into the dock yard and one of the dry docks to see what damage had been done. We were laying next to HMS PENELOPE (the pepper pot) as she was full of shrapnel holes; because of the dam-

age to the dockyard and the lack of workers, the only thing they could do for us, was to fill the shrapnel holes with wood, hammered in tight. We then left dry-dock and proceeded round to Lazareto Base, where we were then sent to Gibraltar for repairs. Upholder was due to return home and we should have gone on our next patrol, taking some soldiers for a landing mission but as we were badly damaged, Upholder volunteered to do our patrol and she went on patrol for about three days before us.It was arranged that we should rendezvous with Upholder to pick up the soldiers after they had completed their mission and take them to Gib with us. This we did and the next day, whilst dived we heard some explosions and wandered what poor bastards were being depth charged. We were in Gibraltar about one month and it was rumoured that Upholder had been sunk. on arriving in Gib and tying up to HMS Maidstone, the fore- hatch was opened and about twelve seamen and stokers were standing on the casing, shouting up to people we knew from the other boats. One of the boats we were tied alongside to was the Olympus, a mine- laying submarine and an old shipmate of mine from Forfar and the Wren, was on the upper deck of Maidstone, Knocke White, when suddenly a flight of aircraft came diving over the harbour and as one man, we all dived into the fore ends. Suddenly realising that they were friendly, as there were no explosions, we crawled out of the fore-hatch giggling like a lot of school girls and the men on Maidstone looked at us in amusement; we were quite obviously bomb happy.
We eventually arrived home to Portsmouth and rendezvoused with HMS submarine TORBAY Gamp Miers VC. was her Captain and was senior to Teddy Woodward our Captain, so she entered HMS DOLPHIN first. The band was playing on the jetty and Captain 1st Submarine Flotilla, took the salute, Pusser Dark and all the dignitaries and afte Torbay had tied up, we followed suit with all the pomp and glory of returning heroes Whilst in dry dock in Gibraltar, it was found that about 70 cells of our batteries had been smashed.
On arriving in HMS Dolphin, the two non-duty watches were given weekend leave, so u to Bromley I go, feeling happy and pleased to see my family again and to tell them of m adventures. On getting off the bus at Bromley Common Bus Garage, I was walking dow Lower Gravel Road, when I met old Mr Dumwell coming up the road. I said "Hello M Dumwell" and expected him to say, I haven't seen you for a long time, where have yo been. Instead he said "What, you home again young Jack", I could have hit him. After m weekend leave, I returned to Dolphin and we then took Unbeaten round to Chathar Dockyard and into dry-dock, for a thorough refit and it was found that the tubes and th tube space was bent 15 degrees out of true and I believe they had to cut the tube spac completely off and re-weld a new tube space and torpedo tube onto her but I left Unbeate a few weeks after she went into dry docks, so I am only going on hearsay.
I was drafted onto Dolphin and after a very short time, I think about one week, I had a 'dra chit to HMS submarine SEALION, the 8th S/M Flotilla at Blyth, as second coxn. Th Captain was Bobby Lambert, I had seen him in Gib and the Unbeaten was well known fo sinking a number of ships and being in Malta, so I was well respected on Sealion and go on well with her captain and all the officers and crew. Our coxn drank too much rum, whic he was in charge of and was a poor old thing and I found I was soon doing half of his jo as well as my own. This gave me a lot of confidence and I was very popular on board, bot with the officers, senior rates and the fore- end men and was treated as a very seasoned an

battle experienced submariner. My first patrol on Sealion was along the Norwegian coast, it was uneventful and do not remember too much about it. Then we went round to the Clyde and Holy Loch to the S/M parent ship HMS FORTH. The next patrol on Sealion was in the Bay of Biscay, down the French coast and Northern Spain, looking for targets but to no avail. The next patrol I remember, there were four boats going to sea together, they were Sealion, Unbeaten (I did not recognise her as she had had her bulging bows where the two external tubes were originally housed and converted to look like the Urge or the U boats with a slim bows), Utmost and Graff, which was a captured German U Boat. The Unbeaten was sunk on 13th or 14th November '42 by British Coastal Command and the Utmost was sunk by aircraft from Gibraltar. Sealion was attacked by night off Brest or La Rochelle, I will explain what happened. We were on the surface and a very dark and cloudy night, our asdic rating had picked up H.E, which we were pretty sure were U Boats coming to go on patrol in the Atlantic. We had six different targets and had started an attack on our nearest one, although we were as yet, unable to see her, when suddenly a huge black object flew very low directly over us. We immediately grouped up and dived but the aircraft returned and dropped depth charges on us it lifted our transmission hatch and flooded our transmission set but our receiver was OK. The next morning, on receiving our messages from Rugby, one was Sealion report your position, which we could not do; anyway four days later we docked at Falmouth and our transmission set was repaired.
From there we went up the Irish Sea back to HMS Forth, our parent ship, after a short rest in harbour, we then went with a convoy to Russia. Firstly we went round Scotland to Scarpa Flow and then proceeded to shadow the convoy, I believe about fifty miles south of her. Our job was to attack any enemy warships that attempted to attack the convoy but we saw nothing. It was a terrible patrol, the sea was rough, we were on the surface, it was continual night and about twelve of the crew who had newly joined us and had never been to sea before, were seasick. The whole of the patrol was about thirty six days, it was terribly cold, we were doing extra watches because of the seasick men, we were getting very wet on look out and the only way you could dry yourself and your underwear was to dry out in your hammock. We arrived back in Holy Loch towards the end of December, after a few days we then took her to the Cyclops, a training flotilla at Rothsea. Our Captain Bobby Lambert, was then given a new S/M being built in Birkenhead and he asked me and a number of others if we would like to join him. So Harold Gill my new run ashore oppo was billeted ashore in Birkenhead, near Cammel Lairds ship Yard, we would get to our new submarine HM S/M SURF about 9.30am, see how they were progressing and off to the delights of Liverpool and surrounding area.
We were billeted ashore with an old couple, he was a milkman about 45 and his wife was about 40. They were a lovely couple, she would worry about Gilly and I and all the terrible girls that were trying to seduce us and he would sometimes take us round the pubs to introduce us to all the dead certs. We would have our breakfast of bacon, egg, fried bread and black pudding every morning and we lived like fighting cocks and at night we would be out on the town, Liverpool, New Brighton or some other place, we had a wonderful time. Sometime after the 12th February we sailed for Holy Loch on HMS Forth to do our working up trials, our speed trials, torpedo trials, depth trials, which was fun but hard work after Liverpool and then at last we were ready for our 1st patrol. We left Forth, sailing down

the Clyde and was met by our escort the White Bear or something like that, after we had rounded the Outer Hebredes, our escort left us and we were heading for Scarpa Flow, on the surface. It was late morning, heavy cloud and a reasonably rough sea, when from nowhere, suddenly a plane dived on us and there were bullets flying around everywhere. We crash dived to 90 feet and I then realised that my left leg was pouring with blood, the coxn bandaged it up for me but it did ache. It was another day, maybe two days before we got to Scarpa and tied up to an iron clad ship. The coxn suggested that I go see the surgeon on board which I did and on examining my leg he ordered me to get my steaming kit and gear from the SM and was to turn in on the sick bay, which I did sending a message to the coxn what had happened. A short while passed and suddenly the Captain came into the sickbay and ordered me out of bed and to get down the boat, "You are coming to Sea with me", he said. The surgeon commander did not argue with him but ordered a motorboat, tied alongside to take me to the hospital ship that was anchored in Scapa Flow. The next day she sailed for Aberdeen and so I was transferred to a hospital there, it was a naval hospital and I was kept there for about three weeks. When I left hospital after an operation on my leg, I was given weekend leave and on arriving in Bromley, everybody up the Naval Club knew I had been in hospital as Jumper Collins and Bert Bonner, also George Manning, who were Royal Fleet Reserve men in their late forties and worked at Northways, the submarine headquarters and had seen my name on a list of sailors that were in hospital. I had not told my father or a girl friend I had in Bromley, name of Joan Surridge, as I did not want to alarm them and they were quite annoyed because they were the only ones that did not know. Joan and her mother and step father were very keen on my company and Dave, Joan's stepfather would introduce me to all and sundry, that I was a submariner and had seen a lot of action in the war and that I was going out with his daughter. on returning to HMS Forth I was put into spare crew and was on the upperdeck, when Surf returned from patrol, as our Captain came up the gang plank, he saw me at the guard-rail and said "Hello Casemore, are you all right now", I said "Yes sir", so he said "You had better take your old job back as 2nd Coxn and rejoin the boat". So I was back on board the Surf without any more prompting. We all had seven days leave and then we were off on our way to the Middle East again with all my old shipmates, Harold Gill was one of them, I cannot remember any of the others names, it was such a long time ago and I think this was sometime in early May '43. On arriving in Gibraltar and tying up to HMS Maidstone, before going to Algiers, we first of all started exercising with the R.A.F seeing if they could detect us on the surface and also dived. Then it was suggested that some of the air crew come down with us, so that they could see our problems and in turn we were offered flights in their aircraft. I first flew in a Hudson, with the R.A.F to Fez but we could not land there as there was a sand storm or something like that and I found that flight very boring and it gave me a headache, as we sat on boxes and looked through a square hole in the floor to the land below. There were no windows in this plane but it was two engined plane and double tail fins, I was pleased when we landed. A day or two later, I had the opportunity to fly with the Fleet Air Arm in a Swordfish, what a wonderful experience that was. I sat behind the pilot and were soon in the air, we went full cut at 140 miles an hour, looped the loop, then did a full speed dive at 170 miles an hour. We were soon on our way to Algiers via our patrol round the Gulf of Lions, I think we saw something but could not catch it as it was too far away and going to fast for us, so we eventually arrived in Algiers. On entering the harbour, the first thing I noticed was a destroyer that had been sunk there with the superstructure sticking out of the water, it had been sunk by enemy aircraft. It was only on returning to the UK in 1944, that I learnt that a member of Bromley Naval Club had gone down on her and his wife still went to the Club but I have forgotten her name.

We did several patrols from Algiers, the Maidstone was now tied up alongside the jetty and there was plenty of night life, ask anyone who was there if they knew the Sphinx or the Half-moon, or the Black Cat; the French did certainly know how to cater for men. U. Bobby Lambert, our skipper, did not seem to be lucky finding targets, I do not remember sinking any ships whilst on the Surf so decided to apply to do a coxn's course, hopefully to be drafted back to England. On asking the Captain, for a recommendation for coxn he said that it will not be long before you are coxn of this boat but I insisted saying that it would be to my advantage if I qualified properly. So it was not long before I was on a troopship, on passage to the UK. This ship was full of soldiers that had wounded and a lot of them mentally or shell shocked, also some ATS girls that were pregnant. Anyway, I arrived back in the UK early 1944 and went to HMS Dolphin. I did my coxn's course, which I passed with flying colours and was drafted to an ex American SM the P556 which was the training submarine for new submariners at HMS Dolphin. We would leave harbour about 8.30 am Monday to Friday and return every evening about 4pm, with the young submariners who were being trained. The crew worked on three watches, red, white and blue but the senior NCO's worked on four watches, for duty PO at night.

I was beginning to become very serious with this young lady by the name of Joan Surridge, so I would do duty PO, Monday to Thursday and go to Bromley, Friday evening to Sunday evening and instead of going to my father's home to sleep, I was offered a bedroom in this young lady's house, by her mother. So I spent more and more time at 181, Southborough Lane, with her and her family. I think I had been on the boat about six weeks, going to Bromley every weekend, when I said to the stoker PO, "will you do my duty watch Friday evening, sony swain, I have promised to take my wife to a dance at Fareham, Friday night". I persisted but he still refused, I asked the other PO's but they were all going to this dance, so I had to stop aboard Friday evening and went to Bromley, Saturday afternoon. the following week the stoker PO was again due for duty PO on Thursday night and asked me if I was going ashore, if not would I do his night duty. I refused, saying I was probably going ashore but if not I had a lot of washing to do. "Well" he said "if you change your mind, the last bus leaves Gosport at 8pm, so if you could relieve me by 7pm, I could catch that bus". Supper in the PO's mess was at 6pm and after I had eaten mine, I got talking to Eric Phillips, I think he was a PO Telegraphist, whom I had known in Malta, in the 10th SM Flotilla. I think he was on the Upright but it could also have been Ralph Teague who came from Shoreham, Kent and I had met him when he was 2nd Coxn of HM S/M Graph the ex U Boat captured in the North Atlantic. He was Admiralty made P.O, however it was because I had been talking to one of these two PO's that I was delayed, otherwise It would have been on board the P556 earlier (P556 blew up at 7pm on the 29th January 1944). Excusing myself telling them I had promised to relieve the Stoker PO, I made my way to P556, on boarding her and just started to descend into the fore-ends, there was a huge explosion, blowing me out of the fore hatch onto the casing. I scrambled to my feet and ran

down the gang plank and started to run along the jetty, when I realised that I should go aboard the boat and find out what had happened. So turning about, I went down the boat which was in absolute chaos, the battery boards were blown about all over the place, with my torch, as there were no lights, I made my way to the PO's mess and found the stoker PO laying face downwards on top of the battery cells. He was still conscious and was saying, "oh my ankle", I turned him over onto his back and noticed that his legs were all shapeless, so I straightened his legs as best that I could and went to put something under his head. On lifting his head up, I noticed the back of his head was all soft and on examining my hand, it was covered in dark red blood. I had already seen the trot sentry who had been on the bridge when the explosion had occurred and sent him for help, so found some wood from the broken floor boards and with some 2" bandages, started to put his legs in splints. After some long time, suddenly people started to come down the boat and a surgeon commander, wearing a bow tie, came to me and asked, "What is the matter with this man", I told him that his legs were broken in a number of places and I was putting splints on them but also the back of his head was all soft, on lifting his head, he said to me 'Don't worry about his legs, they are not important". Within a few minutes he was put on a stretcher and passed through the conning tower and was taken to Hasler Hospital; he died at 3am that morning. On Friday evening I went on long weekend leave to Bromley to my girlfriend's house in Southborough Lane and when she kissed me she realised that my breath smelt bad, so I told her what had happened and she said it smelt like very strong battery gas and my breath smelt like that for three more weeks.
It was not long after the P556 blew up that I developed tonsillitis and went into the sick bay in Dolphin. I was sick for about two weeks, the treatment was to gargle with pomanganate of potash, four times a day. On being discharged from the sickbay, I went into spare crew, some of the jobs I was given was PO in charge of escort duty and escorted several prisoners to prison, with me would be two A.B's. I remember arriving in London and where ever we were going, the train was cancelled, so I let the prisoner go home for the night (he was a London lad) the two escort had a night out in London and I went home to Bromley to my girl friend, luckily the prisoner and the two A.B's escort was at the station the next morning and we carried on to our destination. My next job was to be coxn of the steam pinnace and would often go to Kings Stairs at Portsmouth or other places around Portsmouth sometimes to Ryde, Isle of White, through the buoyed channel, until Southsea Church was on your beam, then hard to starboard and keep the church on your stern until you sighted the pier.
As the summer of 1944 approached, I was then drafted to H34 as coxn, who was at Campbeltown another training submarine flotilla and we would stay out for several more days at a time, also calling into Londonderry and Belfast. This was summertime or early Autumn 1944 and I had a very pleasant time up, there I was also planning to get married sometime in 1945. Dickie Dowdell, my old boat mate from Unbeaten was also a coxn of an H Boat in our flotilla and although his boat was never in when we were, he had his wife up there and so I could see his wife and we would meet sometimes. I told her we had no bathing facilities, so she asked her landlady if I could use their bath, she said I could but it would cost me a shilling for the hot water and I had to clean the bath after use and was told in no uncertain terms, not to use vim to clean with, as this damaged the enamel.

There were seventeen crew members on our H Boat which was built in the 1st World War. After about three months on H34, I was drafted back to Dolphin and then to HM S/M UNRULY who was in Sheerness Dock Yard for a refit. The coxn had already left the boat and he had not ordered any stores or supplies, protective clothing, medical supplies, 28 days emergency supplies, routines for watches, AFO's and all the other paraphernalia and we were due to go out to the Far East. So our wedding was suddenly propelled forward and it was fixed for the 28th November '44. Luckily Sheerness was not far from Bromley, so that I could go home most weekends and eventually our wedding day was nearly upon us and the Captain would only give me 24 hours leave to get married. I arrived home Monday evening and the first thing I was told, that a V2 bomb had hit the Crooked Billet, a pub in Southborough Lane, about two hundred yds from 1 8 1 , Southborough Lane where Joan and her parents lived. A number of windows had been blown out of their house and Joan' s wedding dress was blowing in the wind; 99 people had been killed and about 350 injured the evening before. the next day, Tuesday 28th November, which was a miserable cloudy, drizzly day, Joan and I were married, at Trinity Church, Bromley Common at 3pm in the afternoon and the reception was held at the William Morris Hall, at the top of Masons Hill. All the sailors from the Unruly were invited, we had a very nice sit-down meal of soup, followed by a ham salad and potatoes and trifle for sweet. Amy Phillips was the cook who organised the food and made an excellent job of it; all the food was scrounged. Joan's stepfather Dave, got the ham from the butcher he knew, the milk to make the trifle came from a number of people, who gave up their rations and so on. After the meal was over, the band came about 7pm and we danced and drank beer, which I had ordered some barrels and bottled beer, until about 11.30 pm. Ern my brother was best man, sisters Joan and Betty, Ern and Mrs Fulford and lots of people from the Naval Club were our guests and I had paid for everything; I even paid for everyone to be taken home by taxi, as Dave my step father-in- law told Mr Barnard the taxi man that I would pay him, it cost me £18-l0 shillings and was furious. The next day I had to be on board by 12 noon and Joan, Betty and Vi came with us, hoping that we could get them into the dockyard and take them down the submaine. Mr Morris who was a friend of my parents-in-law and who at our wedding reception, was a Lt. in charge of dockyard security, so this was how they were allowed to get into the dockyard and the four ladies thoroughly enjoyed looking over the boat. They would refer to their visit to my submarine for many years after.

had already rented a room in Sheerness for Joan to stay in but as I was working all day and would not arrive home until after 7pm, it was not much of a honeymoon for her. I had so much work to do, ordering and seeing stores aboard and getting ready to go to sea and then the Far East, as we were told of our destination. On leaving Sheerness, we went to Scotland to do sea trials and then we were sent to the Isle of Man, before going we were fitted with a dummy snorkel. The Germans had invented the snorkel so that they could run lived on their diesel engines and we were going on exercise with the RAF to show them what to look for when hunting U boats in the Atlantic and we were based in Douglas. As we thought we might be here sometime, the POTI and myself thought it a good idea to have our wives to stay with us, so in no time at all, the wives arrived in Douglas. They met in London and travelled by train to Fleetwood, with all the soldiers, sailors and airmen and ad a wonderful time, until they got on the ferry. The crossing was very rough and all the women wanted to do, was to get on dry land, they almost walked by Buck Taylor and myself trying to distance themselves from the sea. However, in half an hour they had recovered and were starving hungry, so we went into a fish and chip shop and they filled themselves with fish and chips; the recovery was amazing.

I spent that night with Joan in an attic room, painted white, it was very clinical and very cold. On returning to the boat in the morning, we were ordered to sea immediately, to exercise our snorkel with the RAF. On reaching the exercise area and waiting about for some hours, the RAF called off the exercise as the weather was too rough. We proceeded back to Douglas but it was too rough for us to get into the harbour, so we wallowed outside; this lasted a week before we could tie up alongside in the harbour and to our wives. I was in Douglas nearly three weeks and only got ashore three times. Suddenly a signal was received for me to report to HMS FORTH on the Clyde, so Joan and I travelled to Glasgow by ferry and train and arrived at Glasgow Central Railway Station about 10.30 pm, so booked in at the Glasgow Central Hotel for bed and breakfast before proceeding to Greenock and then by ferry to Dunoon, next day. We were asked for our identity cards by the hotel receptionist but Joan had not had her card altered into her married name; you can imagine the look we got from her and we were both quite embarrassed. Joan stayed in Dunoon for a few days then went home to Bromley on her own, I got a draft chit to a troopship, destined for the Far East, my destination was HMS Wolfe at Trincomalee. On boarding the troopship. the name I have forgotten, I was appointed 2nd in command to a Chief Master at Arms. We ran the discipline, catering and issuing of rum on board and I had a very active and interesting time while I was on her.

On leaving harbour, our first port of call was Gibraltar, then to Alexandria and I there saw women coaling ship on an old tramp steamer and an Arab sitting on a bollard with a whip which he used to make the women go faster; they carried baskets of coal on their heads. We went through the Suez Canal and anchored overnight in the bitter lakes and proceeded. The next day to Port Toofex and the Red Sea and onwards to Aden. I went ashore in Aden, into Crater City and the Arab quarter, what a dump. On leaving Aden, our next port of call was Bombay, the gateway to India. a lot of soldiers disembarked here, so we had to store ship for our naval contingent and also spent a number of evenings in Bombay, including Grant Road, which was the red light district. Grant Road consisted of many cages on wheels, a part of the cage was enclosed by a curtain and a woman would sit in the open part offering herself for sale; this area was out of bounds to all British Troops.

Our next port of call was Columbo and then on to Trincomalee where I disembarked and joined HMS Wolfe, as a spare crew coxn. That was a very enjoyable cruise, I think I arrived there sometime in April 1945 and the SM Vigorous was on patrol somewhere, I joined the water polo club and went swimming and playing polo daily.

Whilst in spare crew on Wolfe, because I could drive a lorry, I was asked if I would like to take some of the crew of a submarine that had just come in from patrol, up to Dealetawar. So I was sent to the Army Transport base to pass their driving test, which I did easily. So had a very pleasant drive up the mountains, to the rest camp in a tea plantation but was warned that if I came across a heard of elephants on the way, to stop some distance away and everyone to be very quiet, as these wild animals could be very dangerous. Also, if knocked a native down on the road, to take him to the nearest village on our way and t knocked a native down on the road, to take him to the nearest village on our way and to make a note of the time and place and report this accident on returning to the army base. One of the men who played water polo with us on Wolfe, was Mick Magennis who shortly after, was awarded the Victoria Cross as diver on X Craft XE3 into Singapore Johore Strait and sank a Jap battleship Takao.

HMS Vigorous returned from patrol, about the beginning of June and I had already been given a draft chit to join her, on her arrival on Wolfe and took over coxn of her, more or less straight away; the old coxn seemed to be very pleased to be relieved. Our next patrol was again down the straits of Malacca, somewhere round Kuala Lumpa and then over to Sumatra, looking for tramp steamers and Chinese junks but I do not remember sighting any. We went into one or two small harbours and opened fire with our 3 inch gun., to see if there were any enemy there. I remember remaining aground on one of these operations and had to blow all of our ballast tanks to give us more buoyancy but eventually we got off

We were somewhere off Singapore, when the first atomic bomb was dropped; a couple of days later the second bomb was dropped and shortly after we heard from Rugby that the enemy had surrendered. So we then made our way back to Trinco and the Wolfe. I think hostilities ceased about 15th August 1945 and as far as I can remember, we were still at sea, possibly returning from patrol and about the 15th September we left Trincomalee, calling into Colombo and then to Aden. On our way through the Indian Ocean, we came across a huge school of dolphins, they were jumping over our bows and as a number of seamen were sunbathing on the casing, it was almost possible to touch them. When they had gone, our captain said any non duty member wishing to go swimming, should be on the upper deck in five minutes. We stopped engines and a lot of us went swimming, it was said that there was no fear of sharks as they keep at least fifty miles away from dolphins. Our trouble started when we tried to get back on board, we did not notice the ground swell when we dived in, probably because we still had a little way on but when we had become stationary, there was quite a swell and men had to be caught as they were on top of a wave, coming over the casing. Eventually we got everybody back on board, well refreshed with sea water.

We arrived in Aden and stored ship. I remember ordering two lambs, they came aboard still warm and they had brown fur around their hooves. Myself and our T.I. went ashore into Crater City and into the market place, or casbah, as the natives called it but did not stay long as some of the natives were becoming a little aggressive.

On leaving Aden we had a very pleasant cruise up the Red Sea to Port Tewfik and then through the Suez Canal to the bitter lakes, where we anchored overnight in the town of Ismalia. Then on to Alexandria, all of the officers went to Cairo and our 1st LT told me they would be back the next day but in fact they were away for a week. I stored ship and the ERA's and stoker P.O. drew stores for the engine room. We fuelled and watered the boat and I went over to an American destroyer that was moored some short way away, to see if they had something for some of the crew, who had tropical ulcers, as all the quacks would give me in Trinco for these ulcers, was gentian violet. Some of the men who had had these ulcers for some time, the bone underneath the ulcer was going black. The surgeon LT Commander, gave me a tin of solphonamide and told me to clean the ulcer well, then shake some of the powder on and this absolutely worked wonders. Anyway, our officers returned

to the boat around noon and were very pleased that we were ready to sail, so off to Malta we went; don't forget on our journey home from Trincomalee, we were on the surface all the time and what wonderful weather. Malta was still war torn but there was plenty of food now and everybody seemed very happy. I tried to find Charlie's Bar in Sleima, near the old cinema but it also had been bombed but I did find Charley and his wife, also their son young Charley.
We left Malta in very buoyant spirits on our way to Gibraltar and would have long chats with our 1 St Lt, Lt Moore, who was very interested in all the sea birds and fish. He told me he was leaving the boat at Gibraltar and joining Discovery I, that was going to the Antarctic for 2fi years and would I like to join him as he was sure he could get me a passage. I gratefully refused, explaining that I had married only shortly before I left for the Far East and thought it my duty to return to my wife as soon as possible.
On arriving at Gibraltar, we fuelled and watered and stored ship with fresh vegetables, also some souvenirs and I took a big bunch of bananas with me to the UK. We arrived in Dunoon and alongside the Forth*, on the 20th November 1945. I sent the first two watches on leave and Joan my wife came to Dunoon and stayed at the Dunoon Harbour Hotel until I was demobbed, in January 1946. My demob number was 28.

*HMS Forth, depot ship

Jack Casemore

HM S/M Vigorous 1945

HMS/M Unruly

H M Submarine Sentinel, Malta

It was my 2oth birthday 11th November 1953 I was serving on HMs/m Sentinel as a Stoke Mech, and because it was my it was decided by some of the lads, a run ashore was needed.
A few of the names who were a part of this little celebration, are as follows, Colin (Maggie Lockwood, John (Jock) Young, Steve Houlsby, Eric McNally, Scouse Hough, Scouse was a Killick, I think he came to keep us in line, but he was also a near as dam it an alchofro hic, and he was our storekeeper, say no more. There was also my old mate Bernie Warburton from HMs/m Sanguine or Seneschal, I can't recall exactly which.
We started at Sammy's bar at Msida, it was the place to go if you weren't that flush with the readies, but this was on the week of pay day, so we had money to burn (or piss away) so we had Sammy's Thruppeny pint of Toot, yea 3d a pint, it was rough Marsavin with a dash of lemonade, (wouldn't you like to get that these days) the famous Sammy's well famous to us any way, one of them set you up for the rest of the RUN.
So then it was of to Floriana, this was the start of a birthday I will always remember Floriana where the bars were packed most pay weeks, and the Girl Boys were the laugh of the week, mind you they weren't to be messed with tough was the word that springs to mind, many a time a Pongo for instance misjudged them for Queers, to find out they were anything but, Frankie , Charlie, were two I remember as being hard cases, anyway we went on from there to the GUT the most used street in Malta in the 1950s, by the Royal Navy and Royal Marines is there anyone who remembers the night when 41 and 45 Royal Marin Commando, marched on Valetta from their Depot, was it St Georges ?, to avenge one of their lads getting beaten to a pulp by a mob of Maltese in the Gut, a certain Sgt Stanger what a night that was , any one who new the area will maybe recall that it forms a cross and the Marines approached from all directions, Back to the run ashore, I recall we had to have one drink (not colored water) in each bar and their were a lot we got a fair way down and bumped into a gang of our American allies from the Sixth Fleet we were well on the way by now, they wanted to know what was occurring, and was told it was my 20th birthday and what we were up to, so one of their lot challenged me to drinking a bottle of Marsavin without stopping a 20 Dollar bet, it was no contest, I took his 20 note and went outside and spewed my guts up, so then able to carry on to the next bar, we got to the bottom and stared up the other side, I don't know how far up we got, but I do sort of recal being dragged up by my collar loosing my shoes in the course of it, as luck had it some on hung on to them, the next thing I remembered was waking up or being woken up In a dos house, it was Snowies not exactly in the best shape of my life, but we are only 20 year old once, I had good reason to remember mine. I had obviously been to the heads in the nigh because there was a trail of dead cockroaches from my bed across the deck to the other side of the room and I was the only body in the room. Having got back to Msida and on boar HMS Forth, I was showering to liven myself up and saw a lot of reddish bumps, so Sic Bay for me, I saw a Surgeon Lt the first thing he said was, you have been dosing at Snowies, these are bug bites, probably Cockroaches. Serves you right, you won't want to go there again, he was correct, in that assumption, A few weeks later I was in Bhig Hospital with a bad infection which turned out to be Typhus or so my notes said I now th

because I got a look at them when the ward Sister left me in the ward office alone for a few seconds, the point was Sgt Stanger was still in there at that time he was in the next room to me and he was a mass of bottle cuts and slashes from his head all the way down his body,.

Phil Prew, ex Submarine Sentinel, 1953- 1955.
Gatwick Submariners Assoc 1991 - to Present day

HM S/M Sentinel

Naval Towers

Early in the year of 1918, a detachment of Royal Engineers arrived at Southwick and set up camp onthe 'Green'. It was they who inaugurated the construction of what have always been known to the locals as the 'Mystery Towers'. They were built opposite and to the east of the lighthouse. The towers were of a concrete and steel honeycombed with watertight compartments to enable them to float into the required position and then be sunk on the seabed (on the same principal as the 'D' day Mulberry harbours).
Originally they were proposed for the defence of the straights of Dover where they would have been positioned to suspend anti-submarine nets and no doubt be equipped with hydrophones to detect the presence of enemy submarines.
The first world war ended before they were completed, but one of them was towed out into the Solent on Sunday 12th September 1920. It was given a send-off by a huge crowd of onlookers and subsequently became the 'Nab' tower off the Isle of Wight.
The remaining tower was dismantled in 1924 after the Shoreham Harbour Trustees threatened to charge the government harbour dues.

The future Nab Tower

A Visit to Wilhelmshaven

In the summer of 1957 HM S/M Springer made a courtesy visit to Germany calling at Kiel then travelling through the 60 miles of the Kiel canal to Hamburg, and then t Wilhelmshaven where on - July 1957 a wreath was laid at the tomb of the Unknow Mariner, at the mariners chapel, by members of the crew of Springer which include Gatwick Branch Submariners Association Members LSM Geoff Breading and AB Ale Boiling who's path crossed again at a branch meeting after 45 years.

Note Germany lost some 30,000 U-Boat Men during WWII (1939-1945) many of the were conscripted into Submarines; The U-Boat arm lost c.800 boats. The Royal Navy lo c.82 Submarines including X-Craft. The U-Boat arm were the largest part of t Kreigsmarine the Royal Navy Submarine Service was never much more than 3% of t total of the RN.

HM S/M Springer - Kiel Canal

U-363 Loch Eriboll, Surrendering to RAF Liberator

WWII Through The Eyes of Dennis German

I was a (wartime) latecomer to Boats; I was in Malta as a Boy Seaman on the battleship H.M.S. Malaya in 1937, coming back west to Gibraltar the following year for Combined Fleet Man√oeuvres - in the days when we had a Royal Navy!

There, just in time for my eighteenth birthday and upgrading to bold Ordinary Seaman, I was "lent" to the Local Defence Flotilla, H.M.S. Vanoc, one of the old V & W class destroyers -built 1918 and still capable of 31 knots, equipped with the new-fangled Wireless Telegraphy, including the latest "spark" transmitter (!). I had an uncle and aunt ashore in Gibraltar; he was Commissioned Signal Bos'n in charge of Windmill Hill Signal Station (wonder if he had anything to do with that draft?). It was fun being "up homer's" to start with, until I realised that I was being made a convenience of; they waited until Dennis came ashore (Med routine, the day's work finished at 13.00) — except the odd occasions when we had to steam out to the aid of some hapless British merchant ship that had attempted to run Franco's blockade and failed, the Spanish Civil War was still going at that time; almost invariably, by the time we got there they had been reduced to a smoking wreck; otherwise I'd get up there to look after Camp Bay Cottage and Susie their dog, then off they'd go to Spain, in their gaudy "sit up and beg" Ford Cabriolet, known on the Rock as the "Yellow Peril"!

It was after receiving a signal one day, "it is not (R) not convenient for you to come up to the Cottage this evening" when they were entertaining some other brass, I started patronising the bright lights of the town instead!

The only thing I had ever volunteered for - repeatedly, and in vain, was the Fleet Air Arm, which barely existed in those pre-war days; but I had been mad on flying since childhood - and still am; it was not going to be until I was fifty eight that I actually was able to join a Flying Club, and then the (to me) cantankerous little Chief Flying Instructor Sid who could not understand anyone of my age being there, simply made up his mind he was not going to teach me to fly, and he was pushing seventy three himself! I pulled his pisser one Sunday by asking him if, in day, aeroplanes had autovacs, "No!" he barked shortly; "What's an autovac?" asked the Assistant Flying Instructor, a thoroughly nice young chap; at least Sid did know that one, "A system of fuel transfer".

It was only when he finally retired (and I was sixty) that the committee saw to it that I got my chance, but no one got very far with the new C.F.I. they took on; in five years he never qualified one new pilot, he never got me any further than "Circuits" of the airfield, he was so reluctant to take anyone up making excuses of all kinds, in that five years I only logged 27 hours 55 minutes flying time; it. It was only after he had reached retiring age — the year after me, that they learned that he had failed his Medical and was therefore flying and teaching illegally; he was just sitting and waiting for his pension.

However, back to the "Vanoc", she came home early in 1939 - I didn't, I was tipped off on to the "Wishart" that came out as relief; she went home later in 1939 — again, I didn't, this time I was tipped ashore on to H.M.S. Cormorant, a composite-sloop.

That is where I was a couple of weeks later when World War 2 was declared; with this, the old V & W's (and ships' companies) were brought out of "mothballs", and West Country into the bargain - talk about Pirates of Penzance! But out they came to form the 13th

Destroyer Flotilla, and next thing I was drafted to H.M.S. Watchman; the poor old T.I. they had sent out with it, had seen Bleriot flying across from H.M.S/M. E17 in the Channel! well it was not long before they sent him back for a well earned rest.

I eventually came home in the "Watchman" in 1940, after about three and half years "foreign"; I spent the first sixteen months of the War with her, sinking U-Boots in the Straits — anyone seen the film "Das Boot"? then after (for me) two years in Gibraltar, back to Guz, then a spell up and down "E-Boat Alley" on convoy duty between Sheerness and Rosyth, finishing up in Greenock, where my Killick's Rate came through - and me still a "Trained Man", I had studiously avoided Gunnery, Torpedo or Asdics, in my quest for the "Airy Fairies".

Funny thing, I had swapped my "Part of Ship" duties with one of the S.T.'s, to join the Torpedo Party, to get nearer to something more technical; the T.I. did not take kindly to me, giving me all the "shit jobs", in Greenock he had me crawling through the torpedo tubes with rags and shale oil while the "fish" were ashore for their "O" routine or whatever.

That is where I was when a face peered in at the end of the tube, to tell me "Your killick's rate has come through Jerry!" probably expecting me to drop what I was doing to tell the T.I. to do it himself! however, I finished the job off, it was going to he the last time that I did that anyway.

I was duty watch that evening, but my mess mates were not having that, one was sewing a nice new "hook" on my N°. 1's - and no badges! and they pushed me ashore to celebrate, covering my duty for me.

I was made Coxswain of the motorboat, an ancient craft with a bowman under the forward canvas canopy, a stoker on the engine under the mid canopy, over which I looked, standing on the stern benches with the tiller between my knees, and a whistle to give the engine orders; I had some adventures with this, at Imminghan Docks, where the tide almost equalled the maximum speed of this old tub, I was coming alongside the jetty there up behind some Admiral's posh green barge, full astern took ages to take any effect, and I reached out to grab the horizontal planks on the side of the jetty to help the bowman stop the progress and get a hold.

Next thing, the bloody boat carries on, leaving me hanging on to these planks like a fly fortunately I still had the whistle in my teeth, to give the "Stop" signal when the boat had finally stopped, before I crawled along the side of the jetty to get back aboard!

Christmas Eve 1940 was momentous, coming in from sea we tied up alongside a tanker off Gourock to re-fuel, and I was sent on up to Greenock with the important people, to wit the Canteen Damager and the Postman.

Once they were safely out of sight, we tied the boat up and headed for the nearest hostel ry; after an hour I thought it was time to head back.

Down at the jetty we found numerous officers and ratings, having missed their various boats back to various ships, all clamouring for a hitch; I couldn't manage them all, we had quite a way back to go, however I settled for one officer from one of the numerous D.E.M.S. in the Clyde - which is BIG.

Unfortunately he had been in his cabin shaving when they dropped anchor, and bundled off in the boat to get ashore, he had not noticed just where they were; we set off zigzagging around the Clyde, "Is that it?" let's get closer, "No", "Is that it?" "I'm not sure - no", w

never found it; finally I suggested that we had better get back to our ship, "I'm sure our officers will make you welcome Sir".
All the way back to the tanker off Gourock - to find no bloody "Watchman"! "Where is she?", "She has gone up to Greenock, the destroyer anchorage".
All the way back to Greenock, by now I am beginning to worry about fuel, and we had no navigation lights; where is this blasted destroyer anchorage? No sign of any destroyers, I hail a passing ferry - "Have you seen the destroyer Watchman?" "No".
Eventually, by sheer chance, when I have found another ship from which to inquire, it turns out to be ours; it is now mid-night, nobody seems to be concerned, I have always felt sure that our officers never even noticed an extra one in the wardroom! anyway, we found his ship the next day in daylight.
On another occasion taking the boat into Greenock, I noticed something strange about our wake, instead of fanning out thirty or forty degrees behind us, it had widened to more like ninety degrees straight out on either side; I got doubtful and ordered Slow on the engine, just as well — a few minutes later we ran aground on a mud hank! not having run on to it at full speed, we were able to get off it after a while, with Full Astern and vigorous use of the boat hook, then it was a case of proceeding very carefully, while trying to figure out which were the Port and which were the Starboard Hand Buoys!
At some stage we had spent a week up in Reykjavik, Iceland -where the local populace displayed little warmness towards us; the T.I. was taken ill and was sent ashore, I was sent ashore in the boat to deliver his kit bag to the R.N. Base there.
A while later he turned up again in Greenock asking where his kit was! well, it wasn't my fault, I had only carried out instructions.
30th July Commander Hammersley-Heenan was a nice gentleman, and he had decided hat it was time he sent me ashore to qualify for a non-substantive rate; he was prepared to ecommend me for whatever I wanted, what was it to be? "Fleet Air Arm" I said, he went ıp the wall! "You can't have the Fleet Air Arm! We need all the trained men we've got - hey've got to find their own, now what do you want?"
Thinking of what might be the most useful knowledge in later life, I chose the Torpedo 3ranch, and I was duly discharged ashore at Greenock to make my way down to Guz - I vas a Pompey rating but the ship wasn't, so Guz it had to be, but on New Year's Eve, Hogmanay?
n Glasgow I stopped off to look up one of the Wrens whose acquaintance I had made in Hull, during an exciting boiler clean and re-fit period, she lived with her parents in the posh part, Kelvin Grove; a party was in full swing, when I explained that I was just passing hrough, that was not at all acceptable — I was to spend the night there and could go on he next day; Jean, and another lovely girl Jeannie went back to Glasgow Central Station vith me to retrieve my bag and hammock and stow them away complete with trolley on vhich they whoopingly rode, in the Left Luggage.
A wonderful night, with this lovely girl I had just met, whom, alas, I was never going to ee again, she was a student at Oxford if I remember correctly; she got up with me in the norning to get back to the Station.
Scotland is dead on New Year's morning, we could get no sense out of the Left Luggage Attendant who just sat there holding his head and groaning, we found my kit ourselves and

trundled it out still on its trolley; I rushed it to the platform where the train was standing, that wonderful girl came up with an armful of magazines for me to read on the journey and to kiss me goodbye; I had about five minutes to get myself and luggage on to the train, a porter grabbed the trolley - "Get yourself a seat Jack, I'll put this in the luggage compartment for you".

On arrival at Euston I searched that luggage van in vain, I never saw my kit again, and so I arrived in Guz, with a toothbrush purchased on the spot, and the problem of getting myself transferred to Pompey to sort out.

Once there I managed to get a fresh kit, the next morning practically the drafting jaunty had sent for me - Whale Island to qualify Seaman Gunner, "I'm here to qualify Seaman Torpedoman", "Well, it's S.G. now", "Doesn't a Captain's recommendation mean anything?" "What Captain?", "Oh! Alright", and off I went to St. Vincent, previously the Boys' Training School, where I qualified S.T., getting recommended for L.T.O., this was now 1941.

At last I got home on my long deferred Foreign Service leave - for all of two weeks, then the recall for draft requirements; it was to H.M.S. St. Christopher for Coastal Forces Craft; this turned out to be a hotel in Fort William, where I qualified M.L. Coxswain.

Quite a nice little job really, the Motor Launches were sub-chasers with a full load of depthcharges along each side ready for release, and a rather puny looking thing amidships on the quarterdeck called a "Y" Gun, an American depthcharge thrower that fired two charges at once, in opposite directions; on the fo'csle a two pounder quick firing gun, and midships on the coach roof over the engine room, the weirdest of anti-aircraft weapons, a "Holman Projector".

A length of drain pipe swivelling in a revolving mounting, with a piece of bar welded on either side for handlebars to aim it as one stood astride, another piece of angle bar welded on at an angle near the muzzle to act as a gunsight, and a canister welded on to the bottom which was duly charged with compressed air like a submarine heads, via a rubber hose from the Engine Room.

The ammunition for this overgrown airgun were standard Mills hand grenades with three second fuses pushed into tin cans, the pin being withdrawn the firing arm was trapped in the confines of the tin, the whole being dropped into the pipe all same mortars.

On the threatening approach of aircraft, the thing was aimed as near as possible, the trigger that released the compressed air launched can and grenade for about three hundred feet I think it was, flutes cut in the sides of the cans were designed to provide "drag", so that the grenade carried on, leaving the can behind, and thus releasing the firing pin, hopefully, the aircraft would fly into it.

I had an alarming experience one evening, when our young A.S.D. who was nominated if I remember correctly, as "operator" of this Holman Projector, came back aboard from a run ashore well and truly "sloshed", and wanted to play with these damned grenades!!

There was something else that had happened with practically every M.L., they had beautiful funnels like little liners, the exhausts from the two American "V" 12 engines that ran on 87 octane petrol and developed 650 h.p. each, running up inside these single funnels; in harbour flat "lids" or covers were fitted in the tops of the funnels.

There was hardly a boat that had not forgotten to remove said cover before starting the engines at some time or other, and I was told that the result was quite spectacular, this cover sailing a hundred feet or more into the air!
Following training on Loch Linnhe, a crew of seven of us and two officers were sent to a delightful little yacht building yard in Clynder, across from Helensburgh, to stand by the new Motor Launch 232, the seven of us on "lodge and comp" in a very comfortable guest house in that beautiful countryside.
In due course we took acceptance of our new boat and were posted to Longhope in Scapa, the old "Iron Duke" (my very first sea going ship as a Boy), perched on a mud bank, being our depot ship; en route, the most beautiful experience was sailing the whole length of the Caledonian Canal, including Loch Ness, the locks just able to accommodate our boat.
One highlight for me up there in the wilderness, was a night spent as a guest in Tankerness Hall, the official residence of the Lord Lieutenant of the Orkneys and Shetlands on Mainland Orkney; downhill from the Hall was Deer Sound, where two mooring buoys were anchored for the M.L.'s to lay up during the day instead of returning to base, while patrolling the Pentlands during the night.
On this occasion we were running rather low on provisions, and the Lord Lieutenant's daughter, a Wren Officer who was very accommodating (to all the officers in their turn), kindly offered to drive us into Kirkwall in order to get provisions from the Naval Base there.
Accordingly I rowed across in our tiny dinghy with our Jimmy, the lady took us into Kirkwall, dropping me off at the Base, before the two of them retired to other pursuits, to pick the stores and me up later and return to Deer Sound.
There however, we found that the inclement weather that can spring up so suddenly in that part of the world, had sprung up and it was patently obvious that return to the ship was imposs√ible; there was only one answer, to take us up to the Hall, where we made the acquaintance of Her Ladyship, who graciously entertained us.
We had dinner in a grand baronial hall at a table half a mile long, her Ladyship at one end, her daughter at the other end, Jimmy at one side with me opposite; that night we were lent suits of his Lordship's pyjamas, and given a comfortable room each and bed for the night, and a sumptuous breakfast in the morning before returning to the ship.
The next occasion a month or two later was rather different; we had sailed round to Deer Sound to relieve another boat, but the weather turned such that they decided to stay put, we stayed in that night, tied up to our chummy boat at one of the moorings, yet another M.L. came in for shelter, tying up to the other mooring.
The boats were moving fitfully, when suddenly, at one or half past in the morning, without warning, every man jack was thrown out of his bunk by a terrific wallop; it was almost impossible to pull one's trousers on, the boats were rolling that wildly, they were bashing each other's ribs in alternately, and so violent were the jolts that one had to grab a stanchion with one hand to prevent being thrown off one's feet; when it was our turn to get thumped, I could see the timbers splintering inwards over my bunk!.
Somehow everyone got to their stations, they did not need telling; but our skipper was panicking, screaming his head off; the engines had been started, I had rev counters in the wheelhouse, the other boat threw our lines off, the skipper didn't give our quarterdeck sea-

man time to haul the stern rope in but ordered half astern together; I could tell what had happened, every time they tried to put the port engine clutch in it stalled the engine, obviously they had got the stern rope wrapped round the prop, which I duly reported up the voice pipe.

The last order I got was Stop Both, the skipper was screaming his head off, the boat drifted astern with the wind, until we felt the twin rudders grating on the rocks of the little fore shore, it slowly swung around to port, until it was laying on the rocks over at an angle towards the shore.

The order was given to prepare to abandon ship, Jackie Booth our young R.N.V.R. Seaman from Hove dangled a lead line over the lee side and announced "Three feet"; our swash-buckling little killick stoker, with his cockney accent, who insisted that he was Free French because he came from Jersey, volunteered to go over the side first to take the lead line ashore to secure to one of the stumpy little wooden piles, for the benefit of the rest of us. His face was a picture, standing there up to his chin in water, spluttering "Three feet? you!!" "You must be standing in a hole" replied the imperturbable Jackie; and so we all squelched wetly up the path to Tankerness Hall, to knock the good Lady up once more; I took the rum jar with me, as well as my little private 0.22" automatic rifle, but the skipper wouldn't let me issue any bubbly; we were given bath towels in front of roaring kitchen fires, and were each issued with a very welcome "survival kit" of warm clothing, the return of which was never asked for.

We walked back down to the boat in daylight, and after the weather of the previous night I was surprised to see it in one piece; but there she was high and dry on the rocks, and examination showed nothing more than a couple of holes you could put your feet in, in the engine room; they were simply filled in with cement, and that day was spent de-priming the depthcharges and removing the dets from the pistols, prior to them being hoisted ashore before the boat was re-floated; I had five or six dets (that I had been handling very gingerly) left over, short of the cork lined tins that all the others had been stowed in; one after the other I flung them as hard as I could against the rocks, not one bugger went off.

The main shafts were in doubt after this experience, and we were towed to Wick in Caithness, where there was a little dry dock just large enough to accommodate our 112 feet boat. I don't remember what went on, but we finally got back to Scapa.

The officers in these boats were all "wavy navy", our skipper was a New Zealander and I think that he meant well, but he really was back in the world of Captain Bligh; the oldest hand in the boat was our stoker from Grimsby, "Webbie" was a dab hand at sign writing and one day he had got hold of some gilt paint from somewhere, in beautiful Gothic lettering, he painted across the top of the crew's little notice board forrard, "H.M.S. Bounty"; it didn't go down too well in the wardroom!

As coxswain I felt between the devil and the deep blue sea, the Jimmy (referred to as the Market Gardener) was alright on his own, but together, he was the skipper's serving hand and I finally thought it time that I went.

I had been recommended for L.T.O. and that is what I put in for; it was granted, but I had to stay up there until the Enquiry as a Chief Witness; I was relieved and should have gone aboard the "Iron Duke", but I elected to live with the refit crew who took over each boat in its turn, while the permanent crew went on leave; during this period I had a short spell replacing the coxswain aboard the Flotilla Leader with Sir Hugo Brassey, he was a very popular Aussie Lt. Cdr., a grand chap, nephew of the then - what was it? Governor General of Australia and owner of an immense ranch back home, from where he used to have masses of goodies sent out for his crew.

The most uncomfortable experience I'd had aboard "232", was one bright sunny day when we were chugging along with a heavy, oily swell on our starboard quarter that was only just that bit faster than us, giving rise to a very slow, deliberate roll; these "Fairmile" B Class boats had a very high transom stern, with little more than six inches below the water line. Suddenly, an extra big one, its speed practically matching ours, came up under the starboard quarter and threw us over to port, throwing me off the wheel completely, and there we were, because of our matching speed, skating along on its side practically — I thought that we were capsizing altogether, a most sickening experience that I never forgot; the order came down the voice pipe "Slow Ahead Together", I managed to climb back up to the telegraphs and signal the Engine Room, as our speed reduced, we gradually came back upright; "Ozzie" Ozard our little killick stoker told me afterwards, "I was looking out of the engine room port and suddenly found my face keeping the water out!".

It so happened that I travelled down south with Hugo Brassey's crew going on leave, he had provided them with plenty of tucker for the journey, lovely (off ration) real egg sandwiches etc.; in Thurso they stocked up with draught beer in bottles, there being no bottled beer there; I sat opposite a couple of them in one carriage on the train, they were already at the "gibbering gunlayer" stage, on the luggage rack above them a stack of these bottles of beer with corks; the train rattled and jolted over points, and every one of those corks came out, re√leasing a torrent of beer over them, that they barely noticed! I moved to another compartment.

And so, in 1942 1 qualified L.T.O. in Brighton, Roedean School and St. Dunstans, Rottingdean; once again I got my foreign service leave, once again I was re-called after a couple of weeks, and this time it was for "H.M.S. Dolphin, to complete quota"; there were two of us killicks in fact, I remember the other bloke was married with a family, a little older than me, and he told me that he had no intention of going in them, he knew just what to do, half way down the ladder in the D.S.E.A. tank, come up and complain that his ears hurt, which is just what he did, and for him that was that.

As for me, ironically my right ear buggered in 1937, during a high angle shoot at "Queen Bees" (radio controlled aircraft) in the Med aboard the "Malaya"; I was coming down from the flag deck at the end of my forenoon shift (shift?) as S.D.O. runner during a lull in the firing and stopped to have a look at the (then) new secret fuse setting gear on these latest twin 4" combined H.A. L.A. guns, that was normally shrouded under canvas covers; suddenly there was a flurry of activity, I whipped round to get down the hatch towards the mess deck, but this bloody thing fired "CRACK!" with me outside the gun shield, my right ear towards it.

It must have rung for weeks, I was too scared as a youngster to go to any doctor; when it came to my medical in Blockhouse the doctor squinted long and hard at it through his little trumpet, I could have told him but I kept quiet, I had never got what I'd wanted, and I thought, well, this might be interesting.

Then something happened to a big toe, it swelled up and became bloody painful; they wouldn't let you near the D.S.E.A. tank if you had so much as a scratch, and in fact I could not wear a boot or shoe, so I was hobbling over to the Sick Bay everyday to sit around with my foot in a bowl of hot water and boracic powder at intervals.
This made it nice and soft, It didn't do much else; so I finally got fed up with this after about a week of it, and I borrowed a pair of their scissors and a needle to investigate it myself, and that is how I discovered what an ingrowing toe nail is; carefully winkled out, this spear that was piercing the flesh, and it cleared up in no time, though ever since I have had this bother from time to time.
Anyway, finally I went into the old forty foot tank and thoroughly enjoyed the experience, it whetted my appetite for what was going to become S.C.U.B.A. diving one day, that I was going to get involved in after I had turned forty.
Many years later I was to make two Sunday visits to H.M.S. Vernon, to where the old D.S.E.A. tank had been transferred, with parties from the British Sub Aqua Club to try out a "Hard Hat" Diving Suit; on the second occasion I said conversationally to the Duty Officer chaperoning our little group, "I suppose Mark nine Two Star Torpedoes have been superseded now, Sir?" "Hmmmph!" he snorted, "They are museum pieces!" — end of that conversation! !
From Blockhouse to H.M.S. Elfin at Blyth, my day out in L26, and eventually the horrible "Cyclebox"* to be greeted by a snotty little Gunner or Gunner (T) at ten in the evening tired, hungry and thirsty after the journey, who had nothing better to do than rollick me because the name on my hammock was faint due to repeated scrubbing.
The very next morning there was a draft chit for me thank heavens, "H34, alongside starboard side"; but this turned out to be as much "out of the frying pan" as anything, there was this ship's company and complement of officers who had been aboard the old tub for two or three months already, they knew each other, they knew the boat, I didn't fit in particularly with Lt. Oakley, the skipper, who did everything possible to make me the prize pratt.
There I was green as grass as an L.T.O. let alone a submariner, straight from M.L Coxswain with no torpedo experience, to submarine L.T.O. in one easy lesson! my A.B L.T.O. "Tubby" Whorl (now resident in Oz) knew the boat - and made bloody sure I didn't get to know it, "That's alright Jerry, I know just what that needs, I'll fix it", and Oakley pulled me out of the Motor Room, sticking me in all sorts of other unfamiliar places, like on the wheel, with that horrible voice pipe to drain down every time we surfaced, and those strange, unfamiliar and barely comprehensive orders to repeat.
31st July We went up to Scapa for a few days, berthing alongside the "Foudroyant", wooden hulk originally captured from the French and at one time used as a prison ship; the first morning I went inboard to use the heads, on returning to the brow I found it was no there any longer - nor was the boat!
Somebody told me they thought it had gone over to the "Tyne" which was also at anchor up there; "improperly dressed" in dirty overalls and no cap, I hitched a lift to the "Tyne" and managed to get aboard unnoticed - but there was no submarine there, one of the messes treated me to a better breakfast than I normally would have had, but it was going to be difficult to remain out of sight for the whole day that "H34" was going to be out o

difficult to remain out of sight for the whole day that “H34” was going to be out on exercises.

Somehow I managed to hitch a further lift to Longhope - and my old boat M.L. 232, aboard which I was welcome and safe for the day; I didn’t see the officers at all, but my old cabin mate the Motor Mech told me that he had told the skipper of my being drafted into submarines, that he had said “They can’t do that”, but they had!

I managed to hitch a return trip to the “Foudroyant”, getting back at about the right time for “H34’s” return to harbour, around 17.oo, kept out of sight while she came alongside, then sauntered aboard with the mail; nobody said a dicky bird.

Oakley really thought that he’d got me one day, we were exercising from Campbeltown; coming back into harbour, “Tubby” Whorl decided to get his head down on one of the narrow locker tops in front of the port Main Motor Panel; you probably remember that stokers loved to “have a go” at the Main Motors - in “H” boats at least, and one of them asked “Can I work the port Main Motor Jerry?” “Yes, watch what you are doing!”.

Manoeuvring alongside the wall, the crude motor room “telegraphs” - a brass box with three little illuminated windows, “Ahead”, “Stop” and “Astern”, with a single stroke bell to indicate how much of, they went mad, before indicating “Stop” and a voice bellowing down the voice pipe - “What’s going on down there in the Motor Room? Obey telegraphs!” then it started - all over again, before coming back to “Stop” once more!

I looked over my shoulder just in time to see the silly little twit going ahead instead of astern, or vice versa, then Jimmy came bounding through from the Control Room, and there’s “Tubby” snoring his fat head off!!

There was an elderly Cdr. (S) ashore in Campbeltown, and Oakley marched me in front of him with gusto; he was a decent “fatherly” type and was giving me a stern dressing down, he came to “After all, you are in charge of the Motor Room aren’t you?”

That was my cue, “Oh! No Sir” I said sweetly, “Last week Lieutenant Oakley told me that Able Seaman Whorl was in charge of the Motor Room, not me!”

Two jaws dropped, “Is that so?”, “Well, er, um, I....”, I got off with a reprimand.

Just to rub it in though, the Subbie who got lumbered with writing duties, only borrowed MY typewriter to make out MY charge with! that wasn’t you was it, Ronnie Coates-Walker?, I don’t remember now, but we met up in Dunoon in 1993 and you told me that that skipper was no friend of yours either!.

Came the happy day when they all departed, lock, stock and barrel, and I had “H34” all to myself, except for Ronnie, now I had the opportunity to find out for myself what made it tick.

You are right Geordie, they were sheer hell; the Motor Room, forrard of and separated from the Engine Room by a bulkhead, was the junior rates’ Mess, where eighteen of us contrived to eat, work and sleep, on the battery boards which were exactly that, covered with a tarpaulin; there was one hammock (without bedding) slung, one narrow table top, and two even narrower locker tops, barely a foot wide.

The rest fitted in like a jigsaw puzzle on the battery boards at night, overflowing into the Control Room; in my early days I borrowed the Bunting’s large black flag to fold up and doss on in the cold draughty Control Room, the fore-ends were occupied by the senior rates and E.R.A.’s; they had a messman of course who cooked for them and the wardroom forrard there, we cooked for ourselves with a rusty, greasy iron box in one corner, with the old open flat spiral elements, "Tok" switches that clonked round to four different positions, to feed the elements in series, one single, or two in parallel; for ablutions, one enamel bowl, which was emptied through the Engine Room bulkhead into the bilges; where we got water from, I do not remember.

The Officers and Senior Rates had a head in the Control Room, ours was in the tail end all part of the Engine Room, a rusty iron trumpet shape fitted to a metal football, on which one sat in full view, in an oily mist, between two pounding four stage Brotherhood Air Compressors barely a yard apart!

The Main Motor Panels carried seven dinky Starting Switches each, bereft of any form of interlocking, once you had the last one in you could pull all the intermediate ones out; the Main Motors were in the Engine Room, only one each side, so the one solitary Grouper Switch when UP, put the two (110 volt) batteries in series instead supposedly just for the Main Motor feed; occasionally alarming things happened when this was done, the Police Lights suddenly achieving double brilliance before numer√ous bulbs "popped" was nothing, they were fed through a vertical rheostat that someone had to bang down pretty smartly.

I remember one day, on one dive Group Up, the cooker in the corner blew up, another time an ancient disused piece of apparatus - the Fezzenden Generator which stood on end at the forrard end of the Motor Room, started up all on its own, at one time it was used for some kind of underwater sound signalling.

On one other occasion when one of the young stokers was working the port main motor, I heard an alarming acceleration going on as he merrily put the starting switches in, cutting out chunks of starting resistance; looking over my shoulder again I saw that the twit was starting with "fine field" set this time! I lunged across and whipped the rheostat round for tunately there was no wheel to laboriously crank round in those boats!.

I looked at the main motor fuse that side in the Engine Room later, it was a comparatively small frame with ten or so individual strands of heavy lead wire stretched across - and they bore signs of "running"!

The "planing" technique of surfacing described by Geordie Armstrong was particularly apt for "H" Boats; they had no Low Pressure Blowing System whatsoever, they had a hollow "Duct Keel", to which I surmised every Main Ballast Tank had a drain, so in lieu of Kingston Valves, this Duct Keel could be shut off from the sea, but with it open, Main Vents were opened in the usual way to dive except that they were "handraulic", there was no such thing as a Telemotor System, and the steering motor and hydroplanes were electrically driv en, no hydraulics.

In the Engine Room was a noisy thing called the "Roturbo", started up prior to surfacing the report "Roturbo running and sucking!" being made; from what went on, I gathered that High Pressure Blows were used in the normal way, then when the boat had broken surface Main Vents were opened - we had one in the Motor Room, just one on the centre line, wheel overhead to turn to open or shut, and the Roturbo "sucked" the remaining water out through the Duct Keel - and the air into the Main Ballast Tanks, the Main Vents finall being shut before the Roturbo was stopped, the final order being "Flood back Duct Keel"

Crew of H34 at Londonderry 1943

The Warehouse behind was converted into accomodation (with showers) for several crews under training. There was no rationing in Londonderry and Dennis was able to indulge in 6 egg omelettes and other delights.

I was not on my tod for long, I was joined by a complete brand new crew and officers - with whom I was on equal terms, and we got along like the proverbial house on fire, I had a mad Irish L.T.O. Devlin, join me, who did alarming things when "in his cups", and the finest two officers I was ever to meet, the Skipper Lt. Gordon Noll, and Jimmy Lt. Peter Duncan (only twenty one years old, I was all of twenty two), and a "laid back" Third Harry. R.N.V.R. Lt. "Hank" Hunter.
Ronnie Coates-Walker has since told me that when discussing post war plans among them- selves over in the Transatlantic Sheds in Londonderry, "Hank" brought up the idea of buying a submarine with which to "hold up" passenger shipping! in the event he settled for smuggling in a big way, my old mate, Killick Bunting John Gilliland told me that during watches on the bridge with "Hank", he had invited him to join him after the war, but John had held doubts about that!.
He hit the headlines in 1946 or thereabouts, when the new battleship "K.G.5" made a State Visit to South Africa; "Hank" took a Landing Craft over to France and bought up a load of Hooch "for the K.G.5", wearing full uniform to back it up; but debiting the bill to the Admiralty was going just that little bit too far! he was fined something like £10,000 besides a prison sentence.
With their age those "H" Boats were anything but predictable, one morning when exercis ing from 'Derry, the first "trim" dive took us straight to the bottom, the S.P.O. had to pump out two hundred tons from the Compensating Tanks to restore things to normal, and he could never account for where that had come from.
Another time following the night spent at anchor in Lough Foyle it was two hours steam- ing up the river to 'Derry, we went to Harbour Stations to set out on the day's exercises, in that expanse of water it was normally a casual sweeping turn to head for the open sea; but that morning in the Motor Room, hearing the anchor coming in, the normal Half Ahead Together, gave way to all manner of Main Motor orders as if corning alongside a wall culminating with Stop Both and the noise of the anchor going out again; it transpired, after the bows had beer! trimmed down and an E.R.A. had gone over the stern with a D.S.E.A. set, that some plate or other had come adrift during the night, and hanging down under- neath, was acting like a rudder so that the boat would only go in circles! !
2nd August Another most uncomfortable night was spent in the Lough, when with a fast ebbing tide as we came in to anchor, we bumped over the rocks several times, before finally settling at quite an angle, so that no matter where one kipped, he was pretty sure to slide!
Yet another ridiculous occasion when we had steamed right up the river to the Transatlantic Sheds in 'Derry, which was a Godsend, with the bunk beds provided, the plain tables and benches, huge cookers on which to prepare unrationed "nosh" - I remember making an omelette from about a dozen eggs and a pint of milk; but when it became time to return to the other side, I couldn't see what went on from the Motor Room of course, but apparent- ly the tide was just too much for our Main Motors when we tried to swing the boat around and we got wedged under that stone bridge in the middle of town, and there was no getting away from it until the tide turned; we must have provided entertainment for the townspeople!

With the regular runs backwards and forwards to 'Derry, and the "H" boats being 'elegated to training purposes and therefore having empty torpedo tubes, these were 'egularly packed with crates of eggs to bring back to this side; that was fine, until one of he other boats was ordered to fire "water shots" the minute they had got back! .

Now able to take charge I set about improving what I could; there was a small iron box on he bridge with "Steering Tits", little thumb pushes to operate the steering and telegraphs rom there instead of from the Control Room; I stayed up all one night, creeping around ny slumbering mates getting this lot working.

But on the first dive the next day the Skipper forgot to shut the lid of this box on the bridge nd screw it down; it was heartbreaking to see the seawater oozing down the multi core able to drip all over the fuse panel; however, he settled for a dandy hand held steering ontrol on miles of flexible cable that he could take up on the bridge with him.

3rd August Lt.'s Gordon Noll and Peter Duncan, encouraged Wilf Tippet the "Scratch" nd myself to pass the professional exam for Petty Officer; in due course we went to "stand y" our beautiful brand new little Boat in Vickers Armstrongs yard in High Walker H.M.S/M. Untamed

Our first stop was at Myth where the officers picked up their baggage - "Hank" Hunter icked up a motorbike that he wanted brought aboard, one of the 'tiffs was instructed to is√mantle it in order to get it through the torpedo hatch, needless to say, a lot of it finished p over the side!

We heard that during his training period there he had been picked up by the police for iding this bike around with an out of date licence disc, he had given them a false double-arrelled name.

When the Chief Constable contacted the Commander of the Base about this, he said Lt. So-and-so, we have no officer here of that name", but when the incident was related to im he said "Oh! I know who that is!"

was in the Control Room when "Hank" opened his suitcase, and producing a length of auge glass said to Gordon Noll with his American accent (orphaned, he had been raised y an aunt in America) "Look sir, just right for raiding theatres", "What on earth do you nean?" asked Lt. Noll, "Hank" went through the motions of using a pea shooter, "? Oh! hut up!" said Gordon Noll.

was still there an hour later when Gordon Noll came through again, keeping a straight face said to him "I have a better idea than Lt. Hunter, sir", "Oh! what's that?", "A half round ne for split peas!" — "? Oh! Shut up!!"

Our P .O.'s rates came through aboard her during the trials period; Lt. Noll told us that if e wanted to go ashore in "square rig", it was "alright" with him. I felt that it was not only e boat being tried! It was a month of little or no rest and no shore leave, and of course the oor old L.T.O.'s always had the "charge" to see to at the end of the day's activities.

When it came to the "noise trials", as I was still wearing boots in those days, I was structed to walk up and down the Engine Room deck plates while they listened ashore rough their hydrophones.

Gordon Noll once warned me to be ever vigilant with the battery ventilation, he had had xperience of a battery explosion aboard another "U" class boat, when he was, I believe, e Jimmy; he told me how it ripped open the magazine, and the live ammo - brass

cylinders and all were tumbling out to fall on to the battery straps, and he didn't want to experience that again!
I don't remember which boat it was, Gus might possibly know, he had served earlier with Gordon Noll.
At the end of that exhausting period we had our first "Make and Mend" alongside the "Wolfe"; obviously there would be no "kip" in working hours aboard the depot ship, and slept in my bunk aboard the boat.
Getting up around 16.oo for our first run ashore in that time, I went into the cramped P.O.' Toilet in the boat, and felt something very strange as I relieved myself - as if I had bee jabbed in the groin by a finger, strange, I thought, something inside falling back into place
An hour later, tucking my brand new shirt down aboard the depot ship, anxious to ge ashore and have a photo taken in my new single-breasted P.O.'s rig, I felt this strange littl lump like a marble.
What the hell was it? I was scared stiff, but I was NOT going to miss this first run ashore at the same time I went with my hand in my pocket holding on to it, scared as to what migh further happen.
I thought that it must be a rupture and that I must see the "Quack" in the morning, but afte a few "wets" with my mates, I forgot all about it, so much so that it was half past nine th next morning before I suddenly remembered it; I sought out our Jimmy, Lt. Duncan t explain my experience, very concerned he sent me inboard straightaway to find a doctor, think we were alongside "Wolfe" at this time.
The "Sick Parade" being long since over, I found two doctors free in the Sick Bay; I had t "drop 'em" of course while one of the doctors seated poked it about; "Oh! Yes" he said con versationally to the other doctor sitting at a desk, "Definitely operative", "Crikey!" thought, "He's talking about me!"
He explained to me that it was a simple operation, advising me to have it, otherwise I woul be sentenced to wearing a truss for the rest of my life, and that would mean my leavin boats; I thought to myself that I might as well have something out of the Navy, if it wa only an operation!
It was all so hurried, I don't remember leaving the boat and my mates, I quite expected t see them all again, even the subsequent spell of "light duty" didn't occur to me; then I wa in the Royal Naval Auxiliary Hospital, Kilmalcolm.
4th August It was a nice secluded place set in beautiful countryside, I think it must hav been a posh private "spa" in peace time, carved in the stone archway over the main entranc I saw something "Hydro".
Unfortunately I had a cold when I arrived and they won't use General Anaesthetic with an slight doubt as to one's chest, at the end of the week the doctors were narked because I sti had this cold; "We cannot wait any longer" they said, "We are going to operate on you wi a Spinal Anaesthetic".
I didn't like this at all and was still protesting that I didn't want to be awake when they p me on the table; they went ahead of course, putting the green sheets over me, and a litt green screen the size of a table tennis net across my midriff to prevent me from seeing wh went on; then they noticed that I was watching the reflection in the overhead lamp and was promptly blindfolded.

The Anaesthetist, a very nice Irish Surgeon Commander stood by stroking my hair and chatting to keep me occupied, asking me where I lived and telling me that I would soon be on leave; I was still fidgeting with my hands above the "net", I had faintly felt the sheets pulled apart and like a feather tip drawn across that nether region, "Ah!" I thought, "Marking it out"; the Commander asked me "What's wrong, it doesn't hurt does it?" "Not yet!" I said, "Not yet?" he replied, "You didn't know they had nearly finished did you?" Finished! I said if that was it, I could go through it again! and when I saw others "coming round" back in the ward, having had rubber "tea pot spouts" pulled out of their throats, and most of them sick, I was damned glad that I had not had a "General"!

Somewhere at some time in the Navy I had a tooth pulled under Nitrous Oxide because of the presence of an abscess; after what seemed like hours of oblivion I became aware of some twit laughing his head off; what's so bloody funny I thought groggily, what stupid twit is that? I gradually became aware of tears streaming down my face, and other faces grinning into mine, and somebody asking me "What are you laughing at?".

In the past two decades I have had five various operations under a "General" in our Hillingdon Hospital - an extremely close one in 1993, referred to in a letter I was shown, as "a triumph of surgical skill in a case of life and death"; but apart from a slight repeat bout of Pulmonary T.B. that it appears to have sparked off twenty years ago, a "General" seems to have been improved since those war years.

?th August In those days they did not bundle you out of hospital as soon as you could raise a smile and bed rest was believed to be the best healer; I thought it ridiculous for the nurse to bring me a wheelchair after three weeks prone, but it astonished me to find that my legs didn't work when I tried to stand up!

Thus it was about a month later including the week lost due to that cold, that I returned to Sandbank, Holy Loch; I got back about 16.oo just in time to meet the first liberty men coming ashore, recognising mates from other boats; I got funny looks from some, and one chap told me - "Your boat's gone!"

Handing my papers to the Duty Officer aboard "Forth", he studied them then told me "It will be a long time before you see Untamed again".

I did meet my old mate John Gilliland the Killick Bunting, he told me how he had been dragged off kicking and screaming to have his tonsils removed; neither of us wanted to leave the boat, we would have gone anywhere with Gordon Noll and Peter Duncan, the Skipper had told him "You go and get those tonsils out John, I'll keep your place for you, you'll come back to the boat".

At that time he told me an amusing anecdote that I never forgot, though I found that following his terrible experience with a brain tumour in his later years, he had forgotten it entirely himself.

Following my departure from "Untamed" they had gone out on independent exercises one day; "working up" Gordon Noll kept everyone on their toes, springing the unexpected dive; on this particular occasion, nobody remembered to start the Telepumps.

In those "U" class boats main steering had its own steering motor but the hydroplanes were operated by the Telemotor System.

The Control Room Messenger put the after planes to "dive", and when the "Fore Planes Turned Out" Telltale lit up he put those to "dive", the killick stoker opened main vents,

there was sufficient oil pressure stored in the Spring Loaded Accumulator to accomplish al
this.
When the order "Shut Main Vents" was given, this was also achieved - except for N°.1's
the furthest from the blowing panel, because by now all the oil pressure in the spring loade
accumulator was used up.
So when they tried to level the hydroplanes nothing happened, and the boat continued t
dive; Lt. Noll ordered "Blow 1's and 6's", 6's blew fine but 1's main Vent was still open
so up went the stern and they were diving steeper than ever!
Lt. Noll gave the unprecedented order "Full Astern Together"; it appears that somebod
had left some pots of paint in the Motor Room, they had gone over, the L.T.O.'s had sli
on their asses to the forward end of the Engine Room.
By the time they had climbed back up to the Switch Boards, somebody up forrard had shu
N°.1 Main Vent with the hand wrench on his own initiative, it was still blowing, UP cam
the bows just as they had got the Main Motors running full astern, and now they wer
diving backwards!
According to John, at this juncture Lt. Noll ordered "Blow every ******* thing!!" the
shot up, having missed the bottom at 240 feet by a few feet, whereon Gordon Noll sai
"You take over No. 1, I'm ******!!"
Another affable and casual character was an A.B. A.S.D. named Arkwright, with a
aristocratic background, a direct descendant of that gentleman associated with th
invention of the famous Spinning Jenny; aboard "Untamed" he was given responsibility fo
keeping the Control Room clean.
Alongside the "Forth" one day I happened to be in the Control Room, Arkwright was bus
with cotton waste and "Bluebell" when Lt. Duncan came through; seeing Arkwright he sai
"Shouldn't you be up in the Attack Teacher?" Arkwright replied "I don't know, should I?"
"Yes, you jolly well should be - you get up there one—one—two ! ".
Arkwright gazed thoughtfully for a moment, and then languidly inquired, "One-one-tw
where do I find that?" Peter Duncan was speechless, he just gave up and walked off!".
Obviously at some stage "Hank" Hunter had also left "Untamed".
Various rumours and theories as to what had happened aboard "Untamed" on that fatef
day were rife, I picked on the most likely sounding one about a cotter pin dropping out
the log tank hull valve pinion, and for years I had defended the good name of the T.I.
whom the finger was pointed, although he certainly was no friend of mine.
However, since receiving a copy of the official report on the findings of the Investigati
Committee by Lt. Cdr. "Archie" Pitt, that a lady who had got them from David Barlo
Secretary of the Scottish Branch of S.O.C.A. kindly forwarded to me in recent years aft
reading an article written about me in our local "Gazette"; this showed that it was after a
the action of the T.I. that had initiated the disastrous train of events.
This has led me into thinking, if only Tommy Sutton our original T. I., who had trained wi
us in "H34" and come with us to the Yard, had not been taken ill in High Walker and le
"Untamed", that tragedy might never have happened.
As it was, the very first time that we prepared "Untamed" for sea, his replacement sidl
up to me in a very friendly fashion, asking me if I would like to go round the Gyro Compa
with him.

HM S/M Upstart

This marvellous apparatus had always fascinated me, as an O.D. I think that I had got hold of an old Sperry Manual to study; so I naturally jumped at this friendly invitation, flattered that I, a mere killick L.T.O. should be so recognised.
To cut it short, I set the thing up for him, and it gradually dawned on me that he knew precious little about it; thereafter it was the old story, having picked my brains, and finally got the hang of it, it was "F*** off, this is b***** all to do with you!"
I spent a month or two "light duty" between "Forth" and "Wolfe", though berthing party aboard the depot ships was every bit as rough as life in a boat!
One day the "Satyr" came alongside "Forth", skippered by Lt. Oakley, with those of my former mates whom he had taken with him; I stood very conspicuously by the ladder sporting my new P.O.'s badge to greet them, first up were the Jimmy accompanied by "Tubby" Whorl.
I saluted him, grinning broadly; taken aback he said to "Tubby" "What do you make of that?" "Some people know a good man when they see one" I replied with an even broader grin; I heard later that they had tried to push "Tubby" through for the killick's rate and he had failed; it doesn't seem to have been long before command of the "Satyr" was taken over by Lt. T. S. Weston.
Then one Friday I got another pierhead jump on to the "Truculent" — mid commission once more; the boat was empty at the week end of course, I went down to the boat that afternoon and met a chap in overalls with no cap in the Control Room whom I assumed to be the "Tanky".
He asked me who I was, I introduced myself, whereon he threw the ship's keys across to me, saying, "Look after those, I requested special leave, it was turned down but I am still going!" (because his kiddy was ill), and that was the last I saw of Coxswain Tom Gould for many years except when he was "weighed off" on his return!
Unfortunately his replacement turned out to be the sort of mess mate who could smile in your face while sticking a knife in your back, I heard that his previous boat's crew threw him over the side to demonstrate their fondness of him,
This was 1943, after "Truculent's" part in the Tirpitz raid by X Craft, and subsequent patrol's off Norway; once again a mid commission joiner, I was treated like a "sprog" in that bloody P.O.'s mess, so - what if I did have only one badge!
8th August Up to that time "Truculent" was down for "Home Service Only" because she had John Brown's Engines instead of the usual Vickers "T" Engines, and they were watching to see how they stood up to normal wear and tear; but within a couple of weeks of my joining, she was very hurriedly prepared for Trinco' in place of "Truant", and after a couple of week's embarkation leave we were on our way.
We stopped over in Gibraltar while a convoy was formed up, while there an arrangement was arrived at with the local R.A.F. who had been brought out there with the coming of war; we took some of them out for a day at sea, while they took some of us for a flight.
It was an exciting day for me when a couple of us were taken up in a Lockheed Hudson the Pilot's schedule had been to drop target smoke candles on which to subsequently carry out dummy bombing runs, but too many "white horses" on the sea made this impractica-ble, so instead he carried out a mock attack on the "Truculent", it was fascinating to see the spray from her main vents from the outside as she dived.

In the right hand seat up front, I was dying to ask this officer if I might "have a go" at the (dual) controls, but I could not screw up the courage to do so; I kicked myself constantly thereafter!

Then onwards into the Med.; the convoy turned off into Alex, we continued on passage alone towards Beirut, quite peacefully minding our own business in the "protected areas".

Then just at the end of breakfast time - I was having a second cup of tea, "Dive! dive! dive!" I shut off the battery ventilation on my way through to the Motor Room, while two loud "Bangs!" shook the boat and showered dust and cork chips into the tea I had just left behind, and in the Control Room I heard a Subbie telling Skipper "Robbie" Alexander, 'Yes Sir, definitely a Lockheed Hudson!" some Gung-ho pilot who had not read his bloody NOTAMS, who had apparently ignored every identification signal, signal lamp, colour flares, signal grenades.

WO surfaced after about twenty minutes, and the bugger was still circling around, coming in again to machine gun; this time we stayed down for a couple of hours after which he had disappeared, it was probably when we surfaced again that we received a signal from Admiralty inquiring if we had been attacked by air√craft at 08.something.

The passage continued peacefully into Beirut where we spent Christmas (1943) though you wouldn't think so! it was only a few days then we were off for the Suez Canal.

We were joined by the "Stonehenge" somewhere, possibly Aden; I knew young Joe Hartland the T.I., we were "old ships" from the "Wishart", he had been an A.B. Torpedoman, when I got made up to A.B.

They went out on patrol first, sinking a Jap seaplane carrier that all the boats already out there had seen, but been unable to catch because of its speed; sadly though, "Stonehenge" never returned from that first patrol.

I missed our first patrol from Trinco'; somebody had the idea of giving us enough sun in one day to last for the patrol, I think the ship's company were split into two halves for this exercise.

We went ashore at eight in the morning to be picked up in a lorry that took us to a beautiful little beach miles from anywhere, nothing there but a palm thatched hut in the middle of the beach and the jungle behind, there we were left to our own de√vices with corned beef sandwiches and jars of lime juice.

White shorts and shirts were soon discarded, there was no one else there, and we frolicked in and out of the water like kids until about 16.oo when the lorry returned to pick us up; donning shirts and shorts again I felt myself glowing like an electric fire underneath.

I must have been bitten by something too; by the time we got back to the Canteen in Trinco' I wasn't feeling too good, and I fell asleep over my beer at the table.

My mates roused me when they were going, and I felt lousy, aching in every joint, getting back to the jetty I just wanted to lay down, which I could not do on the jetty in uniform, but I prevailed on the coxswain of a motorboat to let me lay in the stern sheets of his boat on hard coils of rope, until he had to go.

Eventually "Adamant's" pinnace came to pick us up, once aboard I went straight down to the Sick Bay; the S.B. Attendant stuck a thermometer in my mouth, took one look at it and said "Get up in that bunk", following which I knew no more.

It was three or four days before I came round again, by that time "Truculent" was well on its way to the billet, that was when I also became conscious of my skin hanging off my back like wall paper! I had just about grown a fresh skin by the time she came back in harbour!, and I gather that I'd had dengue fever, which fortunately is non—recurrent, and having just looked it up, I must have been bitten from four to ten days previously.
10th August One unnerving experience happened when we had not attacked anything and were not being attacked in turn; the port engine was already "out of order" with a sheared off breech end stud; we were on the surface at night, motoring on the port main motor and running a standing charge on the starboard side with the tail clutch out; I was on watch in the motor room with a watch keeping E.R.A. in the engine room, an individual who - when anything was going to happen, was always there!
On this occasion the starboard telegraph suddenly rang to "Stop", and we broke the charge and stopped the engine; the rules stipulated that if an engine was stopped for twenty minutes or more, the full preparation procedure turning the engine over with the turning motor with all cocks and drains opened, followed by "blowing" it round with "cracked" air start feed, before finally setting the fuel levers, fully charging the air start cylinder, and whamming over the air start lever.
In this instance, the engine was stopped for no more than two or three minutes before the telegraph rang again for half ahead to recommence the charge; on the bridge somebody thought they had seen something and they had been listening, before deciding that it was a false alarm.
I had sneaked up to the forward end of the engine room to see if I could hear what was going on, and was making my way back to the switchboard as the 'tiff set to restart that engine.
This turned out to be however, one of those rare occasions when seawater got past the muffler valve and down into the cylinders; when he put the air start lever over, the engine seemed to jerk round perhaps half a revolution, one cylinder fired, the whole boat shook warm sooty water seemed to squirt out of every joint, then another cylinder fired shaking the boat again, this was repeated once or twice more before it subsided into silence, now we had two engines "out of order"!
The Skipper asked for the state of the battery, it was about half charged; the starboard tail clutch was put in and a little telegraph never before used ordered "Auxiliary Motor Full Speed".
Jock Murray my Killick L.T.O. was already there and stooped over the little Starting Switches for this almost forgotten piece of machinery; I later found that a carbon contact on the first starting switch had been bent out of position, but as Jock tried to wham it in the whole thing appeared to blow up in his face! which fact I had to sheepishly report to the Skipper on the bridge.
So we lay quietly on the bottom all next day, while the engine room staff sweated over th port engine, contriving to wedge the two adjacent breech ends (individual cylinder heads either side of the massive broken off stud, downwards against the cylinder, with shorin and wooden wedges against the pressure hull, with loads of emery cloth to prevent ther slipping on the curvature of the hull; it got us back to Trinco', and that was quite some ru from Malaya, Sumatra or wherever I never knew where the hell we were, never allowed t

see the charts; all the same, it was unnerving to see those two breech ends moving up and down each time those cylinders fired!.

And some of the connecting rods of two or three inch cross section from that starboard engine, were absolutely bowed, sufficiently to knock little bits out of the bottoms of their piston skirts.

The safety limit regarding the temperature of a lead acid battery was originally considered as 110° F, but when boats started operating from Trinco' that was soon moved up to 120° F; ours got to 140° F one night on Patrol out there!

Thank heavens we were sent back home towards the end of that year (1944); 1 went ashore in Port Said with a mate, the Killick Bunting, who had to call at the Signal Tower for correspondence, where I waited for him.

A young Coder asked me if I was from "that Submarine", I replied "Yes", he asked if we had passed through about a year ago, "Yes", had we been attacked by an aircraft — "Yes!" then he told me that at that time he had been aboard one of two destroyers stationed there, and they had been sent out to "finish us off" on receipt of that trigger-happy pilot's Enemy Report! they had been steaming towards our reported position for a couple of hours before they were recalled, that was probably when Admiralty received our reply confirming their suspicions!!

And so eventually our happy return to home waters, even that not without it's moments; we had joined a convoy homeward bound from Gibraltar of course, and chugging along at such slow speed didn't keep the diesels happy, turning at about four hundred r.p.m. I think it was set up a diabolical vibration, which shook our Main Motor Switch Panels along with everything else.

I think we were coming through the English Channel that forenoon, I was sitting in the mess very conscious of the sudden cold after what we had got used to; when suddenly the lighting really dipped a couple of times before coming back to normal.

I dashed along to the Motor Room where Jock Murray had the watch, to encounter a thick cloud of acrid yellow smoke; it turned out that the constant vibration because of the low revs, had disturbed the port Main Motor straps to such a degree, that these thick, wide copper conductors had finally touched each other and shorted out, actually burning a large gap in one of them.

It was probably the paint on the asbestos wrapping around these copper straps that was burning, anyway there was a small fire burning under the Switch Panel; probably the last thing that one would think of doing in such a case, but I grabbed the pair of bellows we had in the Motor Room (I cannot remember now just what the heck they were for), but it was only a small fire, and I thought that I could blow it out, which I did do.

But at this point I suddenly felt desperately ill, whether it was the sudden cold or not I never knew; but I turned greeny white, I was shivering and I had a terrible stomach ache, "Dumbo" Oliphant our E.A. turned up to measure up for fish plates to bridge the burnt out gap in that copper strap.

I just had to leave him to it, to his great credit he made and fitted the plates across the gap with Jock's help, having sawed off the burnt ends either side; I could only lie helpless on my bunk, until this strange malady passed off, which it did after an hour or two.

Anyway, it was home again to H.M.S. Ambrose, Dundee, and who should be the duty Petty Officer on the day of arrival?
Unwrapping their "rabbits" the officers left an incredible amount of rubbish in the Control Room; approaching nine o'clock "Rounds" and I am the only silly bugger aboard the boat! Where's the Duty Watch, the Fire Party? I couldn't do it all myself, and when the Duty Officer came down to the boat, I stand there up to my knees in shavings and shit, to salute him and report "All correct Sir, Board clear of earth"; it was one of the Subs, probably lumbered with the duty first night in, like myself; he looked at me, repeated "All correct? Thank you, good night" -Bless you!
As soon as he was gone I went up to the nearest pub to roust out my errant duty watch, but a pint was pushed into my hand, "That's yours Jerry!" well, what can one say?

Yours Aye,

HM S/M Graph / U-570

Bananas!

Leading Signalman Charlie Cook proudly showing some past their sell by date bananas when H.M. S/M Umbra returned to England from the Mediterranean where under the command of Lt. Maydon became one of the top scoring boats.

Bananas were a rarity in wartime England and many young children did not know what a banana looked like. Obviously the trip from Gibraltar though the Bay of Biscay, dived by day resulted in the bananas losing some of their lustre!

HM S/M Templar
Coming alongside HMS Adamant (Depot Ship)

Tree Of Peace Planted as Former Enemies Embrace Beside Galway Bay

In a week which sees the 60th Anniversary of the Liberation of Paris from the Nazis, there was an unusual if somewhat bizarre ceremony of reconciliation here on the shores of Galway Bay last Sunday. A Japanese gentleman, Akira Tsurukame, whose father had been killed when his submarine was blown up off the Malaysian coast in 1944 by the British submarine Telemachus, participated in a simple tree planting ceremony at Oranmore Castle, the home of Commander Bill King, the man who in the heat of the battle killed his father. Also present was a Dutch woman Katja Boonstra, whose own father was killed in a Dutch submarine, sunk by Tsurukame father's submarine.

And if you imagine that the meeting between these people was fraught with tension and old hatreds, you would be totally mistaken. The occasion was shared with Mr. Tsurukame's wife Kay, and their Son Andre, Mrs. Boonstra's three children Patrick, Claire and Jessica; Cmdr King and his daughter Leonie, grand-daughter Heather. It was a mutual moment of warm friendship, relief, and hope for the future. It further appeared to mark the closure of at least one part of the long journey, a spiritual journey as well as one of research, travel and cost for the Tsurukame and Boonstra families. Even though both families are endeavouring to find the wrecks containing their father's remains, there was a real sense last Sunday afternoon that old comrades were deeply honoured and brought the occasion visible peace and joy to the families involved.

The tree, planted behind a sheltering wall close to the castle, was the crab apple 'Everest' Leonie King said she wished it to be a tree of peace. Mr Tsurukame said that he admired Comdr King and recognised in him the devotion to duty that his father shared "I respect you, I admire you, he said. Mrs Boonstra thanked everyone present for making the occasion happen. She was indebted to the hospitality she and her children had been shown. Cmdr King, now in his 90's, was visibly touched by it all. He said he was deeply moved. He quoted Joyce Kilmer 'Poems are made by fools like me/But only God can make a tree.

The Sinking of I-166

It was shortly after 7am on 17 July 1944 when Cmdr Bill King's submarine Telemachus first spotted the Japanese submarine I-166 moving along the surface at full speed 4 miles away in the Strait of Malacca, off the Malaysian coast. Enemy submarines were regarded as priority targets. Telemachus tracked her prey for 12 minutes and when it came within range of one mile Cmdr King, 29 years of ages at the time, was confident he could hit it. In his acclaimed book The Stick and the Stars, he described the build up to the attack: There was a moment's silence in the submarine. You could hear the men breathe while they waited the order "Stand by to fire numbers one, two, three, four, five, six tubes ". After the order to fire the torpedoes shot towards their target, but in fact the sudden loss of weight caused the Telemachus to rise towards the surface. This movement probably caused most of the torpedoes to be deflected from their target, but one struck home with a 'shattering explosion', Five men on watch were thrown clear, but the remaining 88 men including Mr Akira Tsurukame's father, who was the chief engineer on the I-166, were killed.

Strange Odyssey

Mr Akira Tsurukame, was three months old, when his father was killed. As an adult he moved from Japan to California where he met his wife Kay and now lives with their son Andre. He has only one photograph of his father in uniform which was spotted by a dinner guest one evening in his home who happened to be an authority on the old Imperial Japanese Navy. One thing led to another until eventually Mr Tsurukame had a complete record of his father's service in the Japanese navy including the location where the submarine was sunk. Furthermore he received information on Cmdr Kings Telemachus and a description from his book describing the sinking of the 1-166. He read it repeatedly late into the night. I felt I was watching a movie 'I did&t feel any anger. I didn't feel any hatred. I admire the courage and leadership of Cmdr King. I somehow felt my father in him'. Later he and his wife visited the location where his father's submarine sank and laid a flower on the water's surface.

Thinking that was the end of the matter, some months later he was in the Netherlands, and paid a visit to the memorial for submariners there. He knew from his research that on Christmas day 1941 his father's submarine sunk a Dutch submarine. He wrote a message into the visitors book. His name and comments were seen by Katcha Boonstra and she contacted the Tsurukames. Again there was no hatred or resentment on her part and they decided to see of they could contact any of the survivors of their particular tragedies. 'We're just children of these men and its very important to find out what happened' she said.

To their surprise they learnt that Cmdr King was still alive and living in Oranmore Co Galway. An intermediary contacted the Commander who agreed to the meeting. Last March Mr Tsurukame and Mrs Boonstra first came to Galway and stayed in a local B&B On their first evening they walked towards the castle for a look. As they were walking Cmdr King's daughter Leonie drove up and asked them if they were lost. When she learnt who they were she invited them into the castle where Cmdr King was trying to warm up his dinner in a microwave. He invited them to sit down and share his meal. They agreed that night they would meet again with their children, and plant a tree in honour of their fathers, and the strange odyssey that had brought them all together;

Commander Bill King, who lives in Oranmore castle at the top of Galway Bay, often says that if there is anything decent in him, its because he was reared by women; Both his father and uncle were killed in WWI and his mother 'feminine and fragile' did her best with her 'out-of-hand son' He adored his grandmother who in her advanced old age threw aside the genteel occupations expected of Edwardian ladies at the time, and took up sailing with a vengeance In her SO's in sea boots and oil skins she sailed a 54-ft yawl round the stormy west coast of Scotland. She would sit beaming at the tiller in all weathers, 'looking like a jolly red seal in her sou'wester'. As she grew older and there were guests on board she would head out to sea, and if the sea got rough she would pretend not to hear their pleas to return to shore. She's keep her hand on the tiller and do exactly what she wanted to do ignoring the wishes of everyone else.

At 12 years old King was sent to the Royal Navy training college Dartmouth where the day began at dawn to the sound of a bugle and the boys were kept pretty well on the run all day between lessons, the games field, practical training and beatings. At last King was posted to the HIMS Resolution for a 2 year tour of the Mediterranean. 'Such was our nursery', h wrote in his book The Stick and the Stars (published in 1958, and is regarded as a classic account of submarine warfare) 'Between Gibraltar, Malta, Majorca, Alexandria, Athens and Constantinople, the years of our youth fled, and we slipped tardily into manhood, moulded, simple fashion, by the stick and the stars'.

At 28 years of age, at the outbreak of war, King was given his first command, the submarine HMS Snapper, which saw some fierce action in the North Sea5 and along the Norwegian Coast. The midnight sun allowed him and his crew little respite from enemy aircraft. The Snapper was lost, probably in a minefield in the Baltic, but by chance Cmdr King was on sick leave.

The next command, the HMS Telemachus, saw action off the Malaysian and Sumatra coasts where, among other successes; his submarine sank the Japanese submarine the I-166 Understandably, the war extracted its toll and although Cmdr King emerged highly decorated but stressed he found it difficult to settle back into civilian life. He has served 14 years in submarines, 6 of which of which were spent in almost continuous action, an individual record unequalled in the submarine branch of the navy during the war. It was only after some intense transatlantic racing, and a record breaking circumnavigation on board his Chinese rigged Galway Blazer II that he was able to exorcise the tenors of submarine warfare that took the lives of so many of his friends, many of whom perished in horrific circumstances.

Cmdr King was fortunate to marry Anita Leslie, a cousin of Winston Churchill and a decedent of the Leslies of Monaghan, who like many of the old fish aristocracy have with a fair sprinkling of cheerful crackpots among their ranks. But there was nothing whimsical about Anita, however. She enjoyed a brilliant career as a biographer, and like her husband had a distinguished war record. She joined the French Army as an ambulance driver and at times actually drove the ambulance behind enemy lines to rescue Frenchmen from the notorious prison camps. General de Gaulle personally awarded her two Croix's de Guerre. She met her husband during the war when both were on leave skiing in the Lebanon. Anita and her husband came to live in Oranmore in the early 1960's and while she wrote her books, the Cmdr farmed, and sailed, and rode fearlessly with the Galway Blazers. They have 2 children, Tarka and Leonie.

It must have come a quite of surprise when out of the blue a request came from Akira Tsurukame to meet the Commander Akira's father was the chief engineer on board the Japanese submarine I-166 sunk by King in 1944. The thought did cross the commanders mind that perhaps Akira was out for some kind of revenge and he wrote to the intermediary, who was trying to set up the meeting, expressing his concerns. By his brief note we get a picture of the kind of man Cmdr King is. He wrote that he had no problem meeting Mr Tsurukame, 'however as I killed his father, there is a risk that he may be secretly vengeful. For myself it matters not. I am 94. However, at Oranmore Castle I have a daughter and grandchildren. I would therefore be glad to meet this gentleman at any place of his own choosing in Galway. Drinks on me!

Tsurukame and his wife Kay and their Son flew to Galway in March of this year. They were joined by Katja Boonstra, whose father was killed by the submarine on which Tsurukame father served. It was a strange group of people who had their first meeting in the kitchen of Oranmore Castle Tsurukame describes what happened. 'It was almost a miracles encounter' he said 'We talked, ate, drank. We laughed and cried. Three families became one'. This weekend the families met up again, to plant a tree to commemorate their meeting, and to hope their children and grandchildren will never have to participate in the war. They first gathered in Phyllis and Michael McNamara's generous home the Grange, Oranmore on Saturday evening, Mr Tsurukame, a deeply spiritual man, was endeavouring to explain to me why he began this 'journey' to find the man who killed his father in the heat of battle, and to let it rest after 60 years. Mr Tsurukame talked about the richness he has found on his journey but the poet Mary O'Malley, who was also present quoted the Robert Frost poem The Road Not Taken. It seem to explain something of the Mystical odyssey that Mr Tsurukame and Mrs Boonstra were experiencing. And they were all pleased with the poem It concludes: *"Two roads diverged in a wood, and I took the one less travelled by, And that has made all the difference"*.

From 'In Depth'
(Submariners Association Magazine)

Commander King's Submarine 'Telemachus'

Trident
Crew on casing

Lest We Forget

As a tribute to all those submariners who gave their lives in the Second World War, we attempt to publish their names (and rank) in alphabetical order with the submarine on which they were serving.
Research has been undertaken by an honorary member of Gatwick Submariners Association; an ex naval man Eric Smith, who has consulted many different sources to complete the tally of war dead.
This list may help to make it easier for next of kin and other researchers to locate man and boat and perhaps to do further research at the Submarine Museum and other centres of maritime information.
If any reader can offer corrections to these listed casualties, do contact the editors who will be pleased to make the adjustments/additions.

These Will Endure

These will endure when all the hills decay,
When star-toothed Arctic night devouts the day,
And this warm earth, a frozen lifeless place,
Topples to death down shafts of empty space.

In some dimension there will abide
The scarlet of the spear-thrust in His side,
Till time encircled welds up birth with death,
Will shine the truths that came from Nazareth.

Verses by Lt. Com. Donald Dunklerley,
skipper of HM Submarine Thames, lost 1941

Name	Rank	Submarine	
bbott A.C.	Sto. 1	Stonehenge	
bbott C.A.L.	Sto. 1	Rainbow	
bbott H.W.	A.B.	Talisman	
bbott K.P.	P.O.	Talisman	
braham C.E.W.	A.B.	Usurper	
brahams H.	A.B.	Tigris	
brams W.J.E.	P.O.	Thames	
bsolom R.W.	L. Tel.	P.222	
ckery J.E.	Lt. (E)	Narwhal	
ckroyd J.R.L.	Tel.	Narwhal	
ckworth P.C.G.	S. Lt.	Untamed	
cott G.W.	A.B.	Union	
cton T.	Sto. 1	Thule	
dam P.M.	Sto. P.O.	Trooper	
dam W.G.	A.B.	Simoon	
dams A.	P.O. Tel.	P.311	
dams A.E.	Wrnt. Engr.	Porpoise	
dams W.F.	A.B.	Tigris	
damson H.G.O.	Tel.	Parthian	
dcock D.J.	S. Lt.	Rainbow	
dlard G.A.	Lt.	Unique	
inslie J. Mac P.	Lt. RNVR	Syrtis	
itchison J.	Sto. 1	Usk	
itchison T. McM.	Sto. P.O.	Thorn	
itken R.	L. Sto.	Syrtis	
kien N.	Sto. 1	Sterlet	
lbrown R.E.	L. Sea.	Grampus	
lderson A.	A.B.	Utmost	
ldred A.H.	A.B.	Parthian	
lexander A.G.	A.B.	Tarpon	
lexander P.	Sto. 1	Syrtis	
lgar A.E.	L. Sea.	Talisman	
llam H.R.	P.O.	Syrtis	
llan W.	Ord. Sea.	Usurper	
llbrighton J.L.	Sto. 1	Tigris	
llcoat A.E.	Sto. 1	Thistle	
llen D.	A.B.	Triton	
llen D.B.	Lt.	Urge	DSC
llen D.J.	A.B.	Orpheus	
llen J.H.	L. Sto.	P.33	
llen L.S.	A.B.	Tigris	
llen P.R.H.	Lt.	Upholder	
llen R.W.	A.B.	P.514	
len S.C.	L. Sea.	Orpheus	
len W.A.	Sto. 1	P.48	
lerton K.	A.B.	Vandal	
linson J.W.	A.B.	Vandal	
lison F.	Sto. 1	Tarpon	
stin E.A.	P.O.	Narwhal	
ston G.M.H	S. Lt.	Snapper	
nery J.	Era. 3	H.49	
nor J.P.	A.B.	Usk	
nos K.D.	A.B.	Unique	
nos R.C.	A.B.	P.554	
derson A.W.	S. Lt.	Trooper	
derson I.M.	Lt.	Odin	
derson J.	Sto. 1	Tetrarch	
derson J.D.S.	Act. S. Lt. RNVR	Usurper	
derson R.	Seaman RNR	P.311	
derson R.J.	Sto. 1	Unbeaten	MID
derson T.A.	L. Sea.	Triad	
derson W.E.	P.O. Tel.	Upholder	DSM

Name	Rank	Submarine	
Andrew T.	Sto. 1	P.48	
Andrew W.	Era. 3	Tarpon	
Andrews E.A.	A.B.	Tigris	
Andrews G.W.A.	A.B.	Sterlet	
Andrews J.W.	P.O. Tel.	Upholder	
Andrews R.W.	A.B.	Stonehenge	
Andrews T.E.	Sto. 1	Sunfish	
Andrews T.V.	Era. 2	Narwhal	
Andrews W.C.	Era. 4	Vandal	
Andrews W.J.	Ord. Sea.	Tigris	
Anglesea J.	Era. 4	Simoon	
Ansell L.B.A.	A.B.	Porpoise	
Ansell S.J.	A.B.	Odin	
Anstee R.G.	R.G.	Stratagem	
Anthony J.W.	S. Lt.	Undaunted	
Appleby C.H.	P.O.	Unbeaten	
Appleby J.	L. Stwd.	Triad	
Appleby T.W.	L. Tel.	Usurper	
Apps D.	A.B.	Swordfish	
Archer H.E.	Wrnt. Engr.	Spearfish	
Aries W.R.	A.B.	Vandal	
Arkley G.W.	Sto. 1	P.222	
Arkwright J.R.S.	A.B.	Untamed	
Armstrong C.E.	Y. of S.	Seahorse	
Arnold F.J.	Sto. 1	Thames	
Arnold W.E.	Sto. P.O.	Olympus	
Ashby E.A.E.	Lt. RNR	Snapper	
Ashford H.G.	L. Tel.	Urge	
Ashford W.G.	Sto. P.O.	Urge	DSM
Ashton G.C.	L. Sea.	Syrtis	
Ashton S.	L. Sig.	Olympus	
Askew V.C.	P.O.	P.33	
Astley S.	Sto. 1	Traveller	
Atkin G. W.	L. Sto.	Grampus	
Atkinson G.	Sto. 1	Stonehenge	
Atkinson J.K.	A.B.	Regent	
Atkinson L.	A.B.	P.38	
Attridge P.G.	Tel.	Usk	
Auty L.	A.B.	P.311	
Aven A.A.	L. Sto.	Talisman	MID
Ayers F.R.H.	L. Ck. (s)	Phoenix	
Ayers W.F.	A.B.	Orpheus	
Backhouse A.	A.B.	Regent	
Baddeley C.	Sig.	P.48	
Bailey J.S.	Sto. 1	H.31	
Baillie A.	Tel.	Narwhal	
Baines E.L.	L. Tel.	Tempest	
Baker A.E.	Sto. 1	Unbeaten	
Baker A.O.	Lt.	Turbulent	
Baker C.H.	Era. 3	Traveller	
Baker C.H.	L. Sea.	Tigris	
Baker G. W.	A.B.	Usurper	
Baker G.F.C.	Ch. Era.	Regulus	
Baker J.C.	Lt.	Seahorse	
Baker P.D.E.	P.O.	Salmon	
Baker R.V.	Wrnt. Engr.	Regent	MID
Baker S.W.	A.B.	Stratagem	
Baker V.E.	A.B.	Umpire	
Baker W.E.	Sto. 1	Grampus	
Baker W.J.	Era. 2	Thames	
Bakis F.	Sto. 2	P.514	
Ball G.H.	Sto. P.O.	Untamed	
Ballantyne J.R.	Sto. P.O.	Usurper	
Ballard F.	A.B.	P.32	

Balshaw H.R.	L. Stwd.	Thames	
Balshaw J.W.	L. Sea. RNVR	Thorn	
Balson L.F.C.	Wrnt. Engr.	Simoon	
Bancroft A.	L. Sea.	Tetrarch	
Banfield E.	C.P.O.	Tarpon	
Banister P.C. MoC	Lt.	Umpire	DSC
Banks J.A.T.	A.B.	Oxley	
Banks W.F.	L. Sea.	Odin	
Banks W.J.T	Sto. P.O.	P.32	
Bantick W.C.G.	Sto. 1	Thames	
Barber T.H	Sto. P.O.	Saracen	MID
Barford W.A.	A.B.	Thames	
Bargrove R.E.J.	C.P.O.	Oxley	
Barker J.	L. Tel.	Uredd	
Barkley K.	Lt.	Phoenix	
Barlas W.	Ord. Sea.	Triad	
Barnard H.P.	A.B.	Grampus	
Barnes A.F.	Sto. 2	P.514	
Barnes E. B.	L. Sig.	Phoenix	
Barnes M.C.	P.O.	Seal	
Barnes R.H	L. Sea.	P.33	
Barnett A	Tel.	P.32	
Barnsdale C.F.	A.B.	Parthian	
Barr R.W.	Tel.	Tiptoe	
Barrass A	Sto. 1	Rainbow	
Barrett G.J.	L. Sto.	Tarpon	
Barron T.	L. Sig.	P.514	
Barrow J.	A.B.	Thorn	
Barrow W.C.	P.O.	P.32	
Bartlett V.A.H.	Ch. Era.	Traveller	DSM
Bartley A.	L. Sto.	Unique	
Barton M.E.	A.B.	P.48	
Barton S.W.C.	L. Sea.	Phoenix	
Bashford F.G.S.J.	L. Sto.	Snapper	
Bate J.C.	S. Lt.	Undaunted	
Bates C.	Sto. 1	P.32	
Bates J.	A.B.	Untamed	
Batten C.D.	L. Sea.	Tigris	
Battensby T.	Sto. 1	P.514	
Baugh W.J.	L. Sto.	Salmon	DSM
Baxter C.	L. Sto.	Triumph	
Baxter L.G.	A.B.	Urge	
Bayley H.	A.B.	Olympus	
Bayliss S.	P.O.	Regent	
Bayne H.H.	Ord. Sea.	Unbeaten	
Bazley H.G.	Tel.	Seahorse	
Beach H.R.	L. Sea.	Thames	
Beal G.	A.B.	P.514	
Beale P.R.	A.B.	Olympus	
Beard A.G.	Elec. Art. 1	Triton	DSM
Beard R.L.A.S.	L. Sea.	Untamed	
Beardsley A.	A.B.	Syrtis	
Beaton J.M.	L. Tel.	Talisman	
Beattie G.	Sto. 1	Talisman	
Beatty J.T.	A.B.	Undaunted	
Beaumont	A.B.	Tarpon	
Beckett J.	A.B.	Talisman	
Beckett J.D.	A.B.	Thunderbolt	
Beckett S.W.	P.O. Tel.	P.38	
Beddie C.	L. Tel.	Umpire	
Bedford M.A.	L. Sea.	Simoon	
Bedford W.R.	A.B.	Phoenix	
Beecham E.R.	Sto. 1	Thistle	
Bell A.	L. Sto.	Snapper	
Bell A.	Sto. 1	Thorn	
Bell A.E.C.	Lt. RNVR	Thorn	
Bell A.R.	A.B.	Talisman	
Bell E.H.	L. Sto.	Thames	
Bell W.G.	L. Sto.	Tetrarch	
Bellamy L.W.	A.B.	Regulus	
Benfield G.E.	P.O.	P.38	
Bengough I.D.	Sto. P.O.	Trooper	
Bennett A.K.	L. Sea.	Triton	
Bennett C.F.	Sto. P.O.	Phoenix	
Bennett D.B.	Ord. Sea.	P.311	
Bennett F.G.N.	A.B.	Turbulent	
Bennett H.C.	L. Sto.	Tigris	
Bennett L.T.H.	L. Sto.	Odin	
Bennett S.B.	Y. of S.	P.54	
Benson J.	Tel.	Sterlet	
Benson R.	Ord. Tel.	H.31	
Bentley C.A.	Lt. RNR	P.514	
Benton R.H.	A.B.	Shark	
Benz B.	Lt.	Stratagem	
Berry J.	Sto. 1	Traveller	
Berry L.E.W.	A.B.	Unbeaten	
Berry W.W.P.	L. Sig.	Vandal	
Bessell H.T.	L. Sea.	Sterlet	
Best A.R.	Sto. P.O.	Olympus	
Best J.P.	S. Lt.	Spearfish	
Bethell S.W.	A.B.	Usurper	
Bettany A.	A.B.	Vandal	
Bettison K.W.	Sto. 1	Triad	
Betts A.	A.B.	Utmost	MID
Bevan S.T.	Sto. P.O.	Triad	
Bevis P.A.	L. Tel.	Orpheus	
Bewick J.R.	A.B.	Odin	
Bibbs J.	A.B.	P.222	
Bickerton A.	Sto. 1	Odin	
Bickford E.O.	Cmdr.	Salmon	DSC
Biddlecombe W.H.J.	L. Sea.	Turbulent	
Biddulph P.	P.O. Tel.	Orpheus	
Biggerstaff E.J.	C.P.O.	Odin	
Biggleston A.I.	Elec. Art. 1	Triumph	DSM*
Bigglestone H.D.	L. Tel.	Sickle	
Bigrove E.	Tel.	P.615	
Billingsley M.E.	A.B.	Turbulent	
Bilton R.C.	A.B.	P.33	
Binns H.E.	Sto. 1	Spearfish	
Binns J.L.	Sto. P.O.	P.514	
Bird A.J.T.	Elec. Art. 1	Spearfish	
Bird E.F.	Era. 3	P.222	
Bird E.W.	P.O. Ck. (s)	Thunderbolt	
Bird F.G.	L. Sea.	Thames	
Bird W.H.	Ch. Era.	Usurper	
Bishop J.J.	A.B.	Oxley	
Bishop J.W.	L. Sto.	Stratagem	
Black B.J.	Sto. P.O.	P.514	
Blackett A.H.	P.O.	Rainbow	
Blackley J.H.	Era. 4	Syrtis	
Blackmore G.V.	Elec. Art. 2	Rainbow	
Blackmore W.G.	A.B.	Swordfish	
Blackwell H.H.	Sto. 1	P.311	
Blair W.A.	Sto. 1	Regulus	
Blake J.P.	Lt.	Turbulent	DSC
Blake L.	L. Tel.	Upholder	
Blandford E.J.M.	P.O.	Undaunted	
Blane T.T.	L. Tel.	Thunderbolt	

Bleakley C.	L. Sto.	Stonehenge	
Blewett E.J.	P.O. Tel.	Unbeaten	MID
Blondel L.M.	L. Sea.	Triad	
Blyth C.G.	Sto. 1	Narwhal	
Blythe C.	Lt. RNR	Syrtis	
Board N.D.	Era. 3	Upholder	DSM
Boddington R.E.	Lt.	Unique	MID
Bolden J.	A.B.	Porpoise	
Bolton D.R.	A.B.	Traveller	
Bond A.G.	Tel.	Thorn	
Bond L.J.	Sto. 1	P.311	
Bond R.H.	P.O.	Parthian	
Bond R.W.J.	Y. of S.	Unique	DSM
Bonnett H. D.	Ch. Sto.	Oxley	
Boon F.	L. Sea.	Thorn	
Booth F.	Sto. 1	Stratagem	
Booth G.E.	Sto. 1	Unique	
Boothroyd R.	Sto. 1	Olympus	
Bothams P.	A.B.	Untamed	
Botting H.J.	P.O.	Urge	
Boulton B.	Tel.	Splendid	
Boulton J.R.A.	A.B.	Salmon	
Boulton T.A.	Sto. P.O.	Thunderbolt	DSM
Bousell A.E.	Tel.	Union	
Bousfield J.	A.B.	Talisman	
Bovington J.	Ord. Sea.	Tigris	
Bowden H.H.	P.O.	P.514	
Bowen G.A.	Commd. Engr.	Thistle	
Bowen H.W.	Sto. P.O.	Sickle	
Bowers G.A.	Tel.	Talisman	
Bowler F.S.	Era. 2	Grampus	
Bowles H.	Sto. 1	Triumph	
Bowlt B.	A.B.	Unique	
Bowman L.W.	Sto. P.O.	P.32	
Bowyer H.L.	A.B.	Untamed	
Boyce J.M.	Sto. 1	Turbulent	
Boyce V.C.	Sto. 1	Turbulent	
Boyd R.L.	Tel.	Syrtis	
Boyes A.	Sto. P.O.	H.49	
Boyse S.A.	A.B.	Thistle	
Bradley W.M. Mck.	A.B.	Thunderbolt	
Bradshaw A.P.	L. Sea.	Triad	
Brady A.F.	Tel.	Usk	
Brady J.J.	Sto. P.O.	Undaunted	
Brand P.	L. Sto.	Talisman	
Brandon E.	L. Sto.	Stratagem	
Breeds R.M.	A.B.	P.32	
Breen E.C.	C.P.O.	Pandora	
Breen W.	A.B. RNVR	Unique	
Brendon M.J.	Lt.	Talisman	
Brennan J.	P.O.	Porpoise	
Brewer A.C.	Tel.	Tarpon	
Brewer V.L.	Sto. 1	Thistle	
ridge S.R.	Sto. P.O.	Rainbow	
Bridger J.S.	Lt.	Vandal	
riggs E.W.R.	L. Sea.	P.33	
rightman A.A.	A.B.	Sterlet	
rightman L.	A.B.	P.38	
Brister D.	L. Sto.	Thunderbolt	
roadbridge T.G.	Sto. 1	Simoon	
Brock C.E.W.	A.B.	P.311	
Brockbank A.P.	Stwd.	Porpoise	
Brockenshire H.	A.B.	Turbulent	
Brodie F.H.	A.B.	Thorn	

Brodie T.I.	Sto. 1	Stratagem	
Bromby H.	Ch. Era.	Turbulent	
Brookes G.O.	L. Tel.	Sickle	
Brookling M.	P.O. Tel.	P.48	
Brooks B.A.	C.P.O.	P.222	
Brooks K.	A.B.	Narwhal	
Brooks W.	L. Sto.	Salmon	
Brotherton A.	Sto. 1	Trooper	
Brough J.J.	S. Lt.	Unbeaten	
Brown A.	A.B.	Narwhal	
Brown A. McL	Sto. 1	Traveller	
Brown A.R.T.	Sto. 1	Tigris	
Brown C.	Sto. 1	Urge	
Brown F.	P.O.	Tetrarch	
Brown G.	A.B.	Triumph	
Brown H. McD.	A.B.	Tetrarch	DSM
Brown H.E.P.	P.O.	Union	
Brown J.M.	L. Tel.	P.311	
Brown L.J.	Lt. RNR	Triad	
Brown L.J.	Sto. 1	P.38	
Brown N.	Tel.	Turbulent	
Brown R.W.	Sto. 1	Regent	
Brown T.C.	A.B.	Upholder	
Brown W.	Sto. 1	Regulus	
Brown W.	Sto. P.O.	Tigris	
Brown W.A.	A.B.	Utmost	
Brown W.T.	L. Tel.	Tuna	
Browne G.D.	Lt.	Spearfish	
Browning J.	Ch. Era.	P.48	
Brownlie T.H.	L. Sto.	Grampus	
Bruce J.	Sto. 1	Unbeaten	
Bruce R.W.	L. Sto.	Spearfish	
Bruce W.	Sto. 1	P.311	
Bruin W.	Ord. Sea.	Unbeaten	
Bryant A.E.	Sto. 1	Urge	
Bryant L.C.	P.O.	Splendid	
Bryant R.F.	Ch. Era.	Usurper	
Bryson A.B.	Sto. 1	Unique	
Bryson E.H.	Tel.	P.48	
Bryson F.	A.B.	Stratagem	
Bryson R McC.	L. Tel.	Sterlet	
Buchanan J.G.	Ch. Era.	Triad	
Buckie K.B.	A.B.	Thistle	
Buckland R.C.S.	A.B.	Narwhal	
Buckler L.E.	Wrnt. Engr.	Grampus	
Buckley C.	Lt. RNVR	P.311	
Bulford T.W.	Sto. 1	P.311	
Bulger C.	Era. 3	Regulus	
Bull E.B.	Lt.	Grampus	
Bullen H.	Sto. 1	Porpoise	
Bullen W.	A.B.	Parthian	
Bullock E.T.	Era. 1	Talisman	DSM
Bulmer G.P.	Lt.	Olympus	
Bunker W.S.	Sto. P.O.	Phoenix	
Bur W.S.	L. Sto.	Thorn	
Burch B.	A.B.	Grampus	
Burch R. J.	Lt. Cmdr.	Narwhal	
Burford W.J.	A.B.	Perseus	
Burgandy H.W.	L. Sea.	Rainbow	
Burges J.H.	A.B.	Salmon	
Burgess G.W.	Sto. 1	Syrtis	
Burgess H.D.	Era. 1	Oxley	
Burgess J.W.	Ord. Sea.	Unique	
Burgess R.F.	P.O.	P.514	

Burgoyne C.L.	Era. 2	Upholder	
Burnell D.	Lt. RNR	P.615	
Burney R.J.G.	S. Lt. RNVR	Surcouf (Fr.)	
Burns J.	P.O.	Tempest	
Burtenshaw C.W.	Sto. 1	Orpheus	
Burton A.J.	Sto. 1	Triton	
Burton J.M.	A.B.	Narwhal	
Burton J.T.	P.O.	Regulus	
Burton T.R.	L. Sea.	Grampus	
Burton W.H.	A.B.	P.311	
Burton W.S.	C.P.O.	Olympus	
Bury A.	L. Sto.	Perseus	
Bush R.W.	C.P.O.	Swordfish	
Bushell D.	Ord. Sea.	Undaunted	
Bussey F.J.	Ch. Era.	Rainbow	
Butcher C.A.	P.O. Tel.	Triton	
Butcher F.	L. Sto.	Grampus	
Butcher H.B.R.B.	P.O.	P.48	MID
Butler C.W.	P.O.	P.48	
Butler L.W.	L. Sto.	Orpheus	
Butler S.	A.B.	P.38	
Butt G.A.	Sto. 1	Oxley	
Butterfiled P.	Sto. 1	Olympus	
Butterworth R. N.	Era. 2	Olympus	
Buttress H.	L. Sto.	Swordfish	
Bygott R.H.	Lt.	P.33	
Byiast H.	L. Sto.	Traveller	
Byrne B.R.	A.B.	P.48	
Cable R.S.	L. Sto.	Usk	
Cadby C.G.	L. Sig.	Tarpon	
Caddy P.	Lt.	P.48	
Cadogan T.	L. Sto.	Phoenix	
Caffery P.	Sto. 1	Thorn	
Caie E.J.	L. Tel.	H.49	
Cain A.P.	A.B.	Seahorse	
Cain W.	Sto. 1	Triton	
Cairns J.	L. Sea.	Triumph	
Caldwell H.J.	Lt. Cmdr.	Tarpon	
Cale J.A.	P.O.	Thunderbolt	
Callaghan F.	Sto. 1	Talisman	
Calvert W.H.	Sto. 1	Talisman	
Cameron D.	Era. 4	Tempest	
Campbell K.	A.B.	Sterlet	
Campbell P.D.N.	S. Lt. RNR	H.31	
Campion J.O.P.	Sto. 1	Tetrarch	
Cannon M.	Sto. 1	Thunderbolt	
Cannon P.W.	Lt.	Unbeaten	MID
Carew-Hunt A.	S. Lt.	H.49	
Carey R.J.	A.B.	Talisman	
Carling T.M.	A.B.	Trooper	
Carlisle E.H.	Sto. 1	Talisman	
Carlton E.C.	P.O. Tel.	Spearfish	DSM MID
Carpenter H.J.	L. Sto.	Perseus	
Carpenter R.W.	A.B.	Spearfish	
Carr C.E.	P.O.	P.311	
Carr D.L.	Lt.	Union	
Carroll L.	Sto. 1	Trooper	
Carruthers J.	L. Tel.	O.22 (Dutch)	
Carson E.H.S.	Tel.	Usurper	
Carson J.H.	Sto. 2	H.31	
Carter A.S.	S. Lt. SANF	Triton	
Carter J.	L. Sig.	Porpoise	
Carter J.A.V.	A.B.	Spearfish	
Carter R.H.	P.O. Tel.	P.514	
Carty F.	A.B.	Olympus	
Caselton H.R.	A.B.	Perseus	
Caslin M.	Y. of S.	Odin	
Caspell G.E.	Tel.	Simoon	
Cassidy M.	Sto. 1	Tigris	
Cavaye J.	P.O. Ck.	Tarpon	
Cave C.J.R.	Lt.	Triton	
Caveye W.A.K.N.	Lt. Cmdr.	Tempest	
Cawthra G.	Sto. 1	Salmon	DSM
Cayley R.D.	Cmdr.	P.311	DSO
Chadwick G.J.	Tel.	Tarpon	
Chaffe W.G.	Era. 2	Oswald	
Chalcraft R.J.	A.B.	Thorn	
Chalk R.C.	P.O.	Tigris	
Challoner T.G.G	Ch. Era.	Untamed	
Chalmers J.	Sto. P.O.	Parthian	
Chamberlain S.W.	L. Sea.	Urge	
Chambers A.W.S.	A.B.	P.514	
Champion C.H.B.	A.B.	H.31	
Chaplain E.G.	Sto. 1	Odin	
Chapman C.	Sto. P.O.	Unique	
Chapman F.R.	L. Tel.	Undaunted	
Chapman H.C.	L. Stwd.	Tetrarch	
Chapman P.	Lt.	Rainbow	
Chapman T.A.	Sto. 1	Thistle	
Chapman V.F.	L. Sea.	P.32	
Chapman W.J.	L. Sea.	Odin	
Charman J.	C.P.O.	Usurper	
Charnock F.	L. Sea.	Trooper	
Chartres C.F.E.	Lt. (E)	Turbulent	
Chauveau L.	L. Sea.	Narval (Fr.)	
Chauvin M.	Stwd.	Narval (Fr.)	
Cheeseman B.G.	Tel.	P.311	
Chesworth K.L.	Sto. 1	Regent	
Chetham P.C.H.	L. Sea.	Perseus	
Chick J.	A.B.	Rainbow	
Childs G.W.	P.O. Ck.	Thistle	
Chilton G.	A.B.	Sterlet	
Chilton S.	Sto. 1	Tarpon	
Chipp C.	L. Sea.	Union	
Chittleburgh L.W.	L. Sea.	Snapper	
Chitty C.A.C.	A.B.	Porpoise	
Chivers R.S.	A.B.	Trooper	
Choularton J.D.	A.B.	Thrasher	
Christopher H.S.M.	S. Lt. RNVR	P.38	DSM
Christopher P.G.S.	A.B.	Stonehenge	
Christopher T.W.	Ch. Sto.	Traveller	
Church W.	L. Sea.	Grampus	
Clabby J.	Sto. P.O.	Vandal	DSM MID
Clark C.	C.P.O.	Union	
Clark D.	Sto. 1	Tigris	
Clark E.A.	Ord. Sea.	Unbeaten	
Clark E.C.	Sto. P.O.	Triton	
Clark G.L.	P.O.	Phoenix	
Clark L.J.	A.B.	Stonehenge	
Clark R.A.W.	P.O. Tel.	Thames	
Clark W.M.	Era. 4	Porpoise	
Clarke A.W.	L. Sto.	Grampus	
Clarke J.	A.B.	Stonehenge	MID
Clarke K.E.	A.B.	Porpoise	
Clarke R.W.	A.B.	P.311	
Clarkson G.	Sto. 2	P.222	

Clasper H.	Sto. 1	Parthian	
Clatworthy U. W.	P.O.	Seahorse	
Clayton P.G.M.	Lt. RNVR	Stonehenge	
Clayton P.L.	S. Lt. RNR	Untamed	
Clayton R.	A.B.	Seadevil	
Cleary J.P.	L. Sea.	Parthian	
Clements B.C.W.	Lt.	Turbulent	DSC
Clements G.F.	A.B.	Triumph	MID
Clements R.F.	L. Sea.	Snapper	
Cliff D.	Tel.	Stratagem	
Clifford R.A.	C.P.O.	Regent	
Clifford R.J.J.	L. Sig.	Spearfish	
Clift A.E.	Sto. 1	Phoenix	
Close J.E.	L. Sig.	P.222	
Clowrey F.P.	A.B.	P.231	
Cluney T.S.	A.B.	Thistle	
Coakley P.	L. Sto.	Triumph	
Coakley T.	L. Sto.	Talent	
Cochrane A.K.	P.O. Tel.	Triumph	
Cockburn A.	Wrnt. Engr.	Seahorse	
Cockburn T.B.	L. Tel.	Utmost	DSM
Cockin I.W.	A.B.	Rainbow	
Cockle A.W.	Tel.	Phoenix	
Cockwill G.E.	A.B.	Thorn	
Cockwill G.H.	L. Sea.	Pandora	
Codman H.C.P.	C.P.O.	Triton	MID
Codral E.J.R.	Sig.	Olympus	
Codrington T.M.G.	Lt. RNR	Perseus	DSC
Coe F.G.	A.B.	Stonehenge	
Coe-Smith H.	C.P.O.	Regulus	
Coffee J.W.	A.B.	Vandal	
Cokke T.	A.B.	Salmon	
Colbourne W.J.	Ch. Era.	Pandora	
Cole E.	Sto. P.O.	Simoon	
Cole H.E.D.	Sto. 1	Untamed	
Coleman F.G.	A.B.	H.49	
Coleman H.R.	Y. of S.	Triton	
Coleman L.G.	L. Sea.	Talisman	
Collett A.H.	Sto. 1	Tempest	
Collier J.	L. Sea.	Thorn	
Collinge J.	P.O.	Olympus	
Collinge W.E.	Lt. (E)	Triad	DSC
Collins A.E.	A.B.	Olympus	
Collins E.	L. Sea.	Grampus	
Collins E.A.	Lt. RNVR	Triumph	
Collins F.	Era. 4	Olympus	
Collins J.H.	P.O.	Talisman	
Collins L.A.	C.P.O.	Tarpon	
Collins L.A.E.	P.O.	Unique	
Collins M.H.	L. Sea.	Usurper	
Collinson F.G.	P.O.	Triumph	DSM*
Coltart R.E.	Lt.	H.49	DSC
Colton P.G.	L. Sig.	Stonehenge	
Colville J.	A.B.	Trooper	
Colvin G.R.	Lt. Cmdr.	Tigris	DSO DSC
Combe J.J.	Tel.	Seahorse	
Comer J.F.	L. Sto.	Seahorse	
Comfort A.	L. Sto.	P.48	
Compton E.R.	L. Sto.	Regent	
Cond W.J.	Act. S. Lt. RNVR	Uredd	
Conner E.	A.B.	Triumph	
Connolly J.	Sto. 1	Talisman	
Connolly R.	P.O. Tel.	Snapper	
Constable F.	Sto. 2	Union	
Cook G.H.	Wrnt. Engr.	Odin	MID
Cook S.	Elec. Art. 4	Thunderbolt	
Cook S.J.C.	Tel.	Pandora	
Cooke J.J.	Sto. 1	Sickle	
Cooley H.	Tel.	Traveller	
Coombe J.W.D.	Lt.	Utmost	
Cooney W.	A.B.	P.311	
Cooper A.	A.B.	Porpoise	
Cooper A.J.	Era. 1	Snapper	DSM
Cooper J.F.	A.B.	Untamed	
Cooper S.	L. Sto.	Thunderbolt	
Cooper S.G.	L. Sea.	Usurper	
Cooper S.W.	Era. 3	P.32	
Cooper W.	L. Sto.	Phoenix	
Cope H.C.	Sig.	Trooper	
Cope T.S.	Sto. 1	Tempest	
Coppinger R.P.	Lt.	Oxley	
Corbett T.	Era. 4	Stonehenge	
Cordery L.	L. Sea.	Narwhal	
Corn C.F.	A.B.	P.32	
Corneleus J.	Era. 4	Trooper	
Cornish-Bowden E.J.	Lt.	Tetrarch	
Cott G.E.	L. Sto.	Seahorse	
Cotton W.A.	Ch. Era.	H.49	
Coulson F.L.	Sto. 1	Tigris	
Coulter N.G.	Sto. 1	Talisman	
Coulthard R.G.	Tel.	Vandal	
Coupe T.	L. Sea.	Porpoise	
Courtnall C.F.	L. Sto.	Turbulent	
Cousins A.R.	L. Sea.	Grampus	
Cousins M.A.	S. Lt. RNVR	P.222	
Cowlam G.V.	P.O.	Vandal	
Cowton A.D.	Era. 4	Porpoise	
Cox J.F.	L. Sea.	Swordfish	
Cox S.A.A.	Tel.	Regent	
Crager A.J.	Era. 5	H.31	
Craig T.F.	A.B.	Perseus	
Craig T.H.	A.B.	Perseus	
Crane C.H.A.	P.O.	Thunderbolt	
Crane G.	P.O.	Parthian	
Craw A.M.	A.B.	Perseus	
Crawley-Boevey T.R.	S. Lt.	Tigris	
Crean W.J.	L. Sto.	Swordfish	
Cringle J.	S. Lt. RNR	Narwhal	
Cripps R.V.	Era. 2	H.49	MID
Critchell W.J.G.	L. Sea.	Orpheus	
Croker R.J.	Sto. 1	Splendid	
Crompton T.	A.B.	Thorn	
Crone J.S.	Surg. Lt. RNVR	Sterlet	
Cronin A.J.	A.B.	Tempest	
Crook F.C.	A.B.	Sickle	
Crosby V.J.	L. Tel.	Saracen	
Cross C.M.	S. Lt. RNVR	Simoon	
Cross E.K.	Wrnt. Engr.	Orpheus	
Cross G.H.	A.B.	Triumph	
Cross R.W.B.	P.O.	Odin	
Crossland F.	Tel.	Trooper	
Crouch C.B.	Lt. Cmdr.	Thunderbolt	DSO
Crouch J.E.	P.O.	Odin	
Crouchman V.P.T.	A.B.	Porpoise	
Crowe F..	L. Sea.	Olympus	
Crowston A.S.	Era. 3	Turbulent	DSM*
Crowther R.	L. Sea.	Stonehenge	
Cruickshank J.A.	Era. 3	Usk	

Crummey R.T.	Tel.	Triumph	DSM*
Crump R.C.	L. Sto.	Rainbow	
Cryle A.M.	Era. 3	Grampus	
Cucknell A.	Tel.	Stonehenge	
Culbert W.D.	Era. 3	Tigris	
Culham J.W.S.	Lt.	Regent	
Cullingford G.B.	L. Sea.	Triad	
Cummings A.	Sto. 1	Thames	
Cunningham H.	L. Sto.	Thames	
Cunningham R.L.	Lt.	P.333	
Cunningham W.N.	Sto. P.O.	P.514	
Cunningham W.N.	Sto. P.O.	P.615	
Currell R.E.W.	Sto. 1	Parthian	
Currie F.B.	Lt. Cmdr.	Regulus	
Curry T.	P.O.	Thunderbolt	
Curry T.A.	L. Sto.	Trooper	
Curtis G.W.	Ch. Era.	Thunderbolt	DSM
Curtis H.W.	P.O.	Thames	
Cusack S.J.G.	Era. 1	P.222	
Cuthbert A.W.E.	L. Sig.	Sickle	
Cuthbert G.	L. Sto.	Grampus	
Daft A.J.	Sto. 1	P.615	
D'Almaine	Lt.	Undaunted	MID
Daly M.A.	Sto. 1	Thunderbolt	
Dance J.W.	Era. 2	Orpheus	
Dando T.J.B.	P.O.	Swordfish	
Danks G.V.	Era. 4	Untamed	
Darbyshire V.L.	Lt.	Usk	
Darch E.J.	L. Sto.	Spearfish	
Darling C.	Sto. 1	Turbulent	MID
Darling G.P.	Lt.	Usk	
Daruty M.	Sto. 2	Narval (Fr.)	
Davey A.J.	P.O.	Olympus	
Davidson J.H.	C.P.O.	H.49	
Davidson J.K.	A.B.	Tarpon	
Davidson R.W.	L. Sea.	Upholder	DSM
Davidson W.	P.O. Tel.	Sickle	
Davies A.E.	L. Sea.	Triumph	
Davies A.F.	Lt.	P.615	
Davies C.T.	Lt.	Orpheus	
Davies E.W.	L. Sto.	Sickle	
Davies G.W.	Sto. 2	Tempest	
Davies G.Y.	Sto. 1	Trooper	
Davies H.	A.B.	Tetrarch	
Davies H.	L. Sig.	Swordfish	MID
Davies J.	Sto. 1	Thistle	
Davies J.I.M.	L. Sea.	Usk	
Davies L.F.	Wrnt. Engr.	Thorn	
Davies M.E.	P.O. Tel.	Usurper	DSM
Davies T.B.	A.B.	Usurper	
Davies T.E.	Sto. 1	Tarpon	
Davies T.W.	Sto. 1	Tarpon	
Davies W.J.	Era. 4	Tetrarch	
Davis C.V.	Sto P.O.	Traveller	
Davis F.J.	Sto. P.O.	Regulus	
Davis H.E.	Sto. 1	Oxley	
Davis H.J.	Sto. 1	Narwhal	
Davis M.H.	Lt.	Rainbow	
Davis W.B.	P.O.	Olympus	
Davis W.J.	P.O.	Phoenix	
Davis W.L.	Wrnt. Engr.	Salmon	
Davis W.T.	Sto. 1	Olympus	
Davison A.S.	A.B.	Utmost	
Davison R.	A.B.	Urge	

Daw W.S.	Sig.	Narwhal	
Dawson P.R.	Sto. 1	Olympus	
Dawson R.	C.P.O.	Odin	
Dawson W.J.	Sto. 1	P.514	
Day F.	A.B.	Urge	
Day H.C.	Sig.	Simoon	
Day J.R.	P.O.	Triton	
Day T.H.	A.B.	P.48	
Deackes R.A.	Ord. Sea.	Triumph	
Deacon B.F.	Ch. Era.	Odin	
Deacon H.J.	P.O.	Perseus	
Deakin R.	Sto. P.O.	P.222	
Dean A.J.	P.O.	Traveller	
Dean E.	L. Sto.	Thames	
Dean H.	S. Lt.	Triad	
Dean P.C.	Sto. 1	Utmost	
Dean R.E.	Lt. RNR	Triton	MID
Dean W.H.	Era. 2	Triton	
Dearden L.H.L.	S. Lt.	H.49	
Dearn A.S.A.	P.O.	Snapper	
Deary R.	A.B.	Talisman	
Dee J.C.	Sto. 1	Phoenix	
Deeley S.	Sto. 1	Tetrarch	
Deller J.A.	A.B.	Turbulent	
Deller W.G.A.	L. Sea.	Traveller	
Delussey A.	Sto. 1	Spearfish	
Dempster D.	Sto. 1	Tigris	
Dempster W.A.	Era. 4	Triumph	
Denby E.	P.O.	Parthian	
Denne A.E.J.	L. Sto.	Unique	MID
Denne B.H.	Sto. 1	Syrtis	
Denner W.F.J.	C.P.O.	Narwhal	
Dennis F.	P.O.	Parthian	
Dennis R.A.	L. Tel.	Turbulent	
Dennison G.	A.B.	Thames	
Denyer C.J.	A.B.	Grampus	
Des Voeux J.H.	S. Lt.	Utmost	
Detton F.C.	L. Sto.	Thorn	
Dewhurst H.E.	A.B.	Regent	
Dicker R.	P.O.	Oxley	
Dickerson R.F.	Ord. Tel.	Perseus	
Dickerson S.J.	Sto. 1	Stratagem	
Dickinson R.	L. Sto.	Traveller	
Dickson G.	L. Sto.	P.514	
Dickson J. McD.	Sto. 1	Perseus	
Diggens G.A.	P.O. Tel.	Phoenix	
Dinsdale G.A.	Sto. 1	P.615	
Dixon F.E.P.	L. Tel.	Sterlet	
Dixon G.	L. Sto.	Salmon	
Dixon J.	Sto. 1	Thistle	
Dixon S.H.	C.P.O.	Splendid	
Dixon T.	A.B.	Rainbow	
Dobbie R.	A.B.	Snapper	
Dobson G.	L. Sea.	Perseus	
Dodd K.	L. Sea.	Thorn	
Dodson R.A.W.	Tel.	Snapper	
Dodson T.	L. Sto.	Vandal	
Doffman R.	Era. 4	Sanguine	
Dolling R.W.	L. Sto.	Thistle	
Dolton L.H.	L. Sto.	Orpheus	
Don R.W.G.	Lt.	Triumph	DSC**
Donachy J.	A.B.	Tigris	
Donohue P.J.	Sto. P.O.	P.311	
Doran E.J.	A.B.	Parthian	

Doran L.H.	Era. 2	P.33	
Dorrell K.J.	Lt.	Grampus	
Doucy C.A.	A.B.	Snapper	
Doughty H.	A.B.	H.31	
Doughty W.G.	Sto. 1	Thunderbolt	
Douglas A.A.B.	A.B.	Sceptre	
Douglas W.C.	L. Stwd.	Tigris	MID
Dover W.A.	Sig.	Oxley	
Dow J.	Tel.	Untamed	
Dowdell F.H.G.	Tel.	H.31	
Dowdie T.G.	L. Sto.	Vandal	
Dowen J.W.	A.B.	Saracen	
Dowler C.G.	A.B.	P.33	
Dowling B.	Sto. P.O.	Thames	
Down C.S.T.	Sto. 1	Turbulent	
Down H.G.	A.B.	Triton	
Down P.L.J.	Era. 3	P.311	
Downham A.E.	Era. 4	Thunderbolt	
Dracup D.G.R.	Sto. 1	Stratagem	
Drake R.F.	S. Lt.	Stonehenge	MID
Draper A.D.	Sto. P.O.	Porpoise	DSM
Drew F.	Sig.	Tempest	
Drew V.H.F.	Lt. RNVR	Porpoise	
Drew W.E.S.	Tel.	Thistle	
Drummond J.R.	Lt.	Sickle	DSO DSC
Drysdale I. McN. A.	Surg. Lt.	Phoenix	
Duckham H.R.	C.P.O. Tel.	Narwhal	
Dudd P.C.G.	A.B.	Regulus	
Dudgon E.	Era. 4	P.48	
Duell G.A.	P.O. Ck. (s)	Perseus	
Duffay C.G.H.	P.O.	Triumph	DSM
Duffay O.V.H.	P.O.	Regulus	
Duffy J.A.	L. Sea.	Umpire	
Duffy M.B.J.	P.O.	Tigris	MID
Duncan A.D. McG.	Sto. 1	Sickle	
Duncan J.P.	Lt.	Untamed	
Dunford W.E.	L. Sea.	Triad	
Dunkerley W.D.	Lt. Cmdr.	Thames	
Dunkey G.	A.B.	Sceptre	
Dunkinson F.W.G.	P.O.	P.222	
Dunlop E.	P.O.	Triad	
Dunn E.J.	A.B.	Triad	
Dunn H.	P.O.	Sterlet	
Dunn J.F.	L. Ck.	Rainbow	
Dunstane W.A.C.J.	Era. 4	Triad	
Dunstone D.H.	Tel.	Sickle	
Dunwell J.	L. Sea.	Seahorse	
Durcan A.P.	P.O.	Salmon	
Durnell. C.W.	Era. 5	P.38	BEM
Dyall W.F.	A.B.	Porpoise	
Dye W.E.	P.O.	P.311	
Dye W.J.	Sto. 1	Turbulent	
Dyer A.H.	A.B.	Thames	
Dymott H.G.	Lt. Cmdr.	Olympus	
Dyson A.	L. Sto.	P.615	
Eales R.C.	A.B.	Tempest	
Earl G.D.	A.B.	Rainbow	
Earles R.S.	L. Sea.	Vandal	
Earley S.J.	Era. 4	Upstart	
Early A.H.	Era. 2	Triton	
Earwaker A.E.G.	A.B.	Narwhal	
Eason W.J.	C.P.O.	Thorn	
East A.	Sto. P.O.	Usk	
East C.M.	L. Tel.	Triton	
Eaton R.M.P.	Lt.	Tigris	
Ebel M.V.	Lt. RNVR	Vandal	GM
Eccles J.	Tel.	Triad	
Edden C.H.	L. Ck.	Triad	
Eddy W.J.	A.B.	Union	
Edgar J.	Lt.	Thunderbolt	
Edgar S.M.	Sto. 1	Unique	
Edmonds C.W.	A.B.	H.49	
Edmonds H.N.	Lt.	P.36	
Edmunds H.W.H.F.	Elec. Art. 3	Olympus	
Edmunds R.A.	Lt. RNVR	P.216	
Edney A.A.	Elec. Art. 1	Triad	DSM
Edom G.A.	P.O.	Rainbow	
Edwards A.	Sto. P.O.	P.556	
Edwards D.L.	A.B.	Stonehenge	
Edwards E.P.	Sto. P.O.	Grampus	
Edwards E.R.	P.O.	Sickle	
Edwards G.	L. Sto.	Odin	
Edwards H.	A.B.	Stonehenge	
Edwards H.	L. Sto.	P.32	
Edwards J.	A.B.	Rainbow	
Edwards L.	Sto. P.O.	Thames	
Edwards L.G.	A.B.	P.615	
Edwards W.G.	L. Tel.	Porpoise	
Edwell E.R.	L. Sea.	P.38	
Eldridge H.A.	Tel.	Usurper	
Eldridge W.J.E.	L. Sto.	Seahorse	
Eliot R.D.	Sto. 1	Oswald	
Ellgood H.	A.B.	Traveller	
Ellin S.	P.O. Tel.	Simoon	
Elliott C.S.	P.O.	Thunderbolt	
Elliott J.	Ch. Era.	Tetrarch	DSM
Elliott R.	A.B.	Simoon	
Elliott R.C.	S. Lt. RNR	Saracen	
Ellis G.E.	A.B.	Olympus	
Ellis G.G.	P.O.	Regent	
Ellis J.D.	L. Sto.	Truant	
Ellis R.Y.D.	Elec. Art. 4	Traveller	
Ellis S.	L. Sto.	Rainbow	
Ellison J.W.	L. Tel.	Orpheus	
Ellwood R.	A.B.	Sterlet	
Elnor E.	Sto. 1	Parthian	
Elphick C.D.	P.O. Tel.	Thorn	
Elvin H.C.	L. Sto.	Narwhal	
Endersby S.C.	P.O.	Tarpon	
England E.G.	Elec. Art. 3	Sahib	
England G.A.	A.B.	Perseus	
England L.N.	A.B.	P.514	
Ennis H.P.	A.B.	Stonehenge	
Ennor R.P.N.	Lt. RNR	Thistle	
Ensby A.E.	A.B.	H.31	
Errington C.W.J.	A.B.	Upright	
Esau L.W.	A.B.	Triumph	
Ethell F.	L. Tel.	Parthian	
Etheridge G.D.	Era. 1	Tarpon	
Eustace D.A.	Lt.	P.38	
Evans A.E.	L. Sto.	Sickle	
Evans C.W.	A.B.	P.311	
Evans E.R.	A.B.	Tetrarch	
Evans J.	L. Sig.	Orpheus	
Evans J.M.	Sto. 1	Triad	
Evans L.G.	A.B.	P.222	
Evans M.A.	Sto. 1	Spearfish	
Evans W.E.	S. Lt. RNR	Tetrarch	MID

Evans W.E.H.	Era. 3	Sterlet		Forsyth H.G.	A.B.	Syrtis	
Evans W.G.F.	L. Stwd.	Thistle		Foster A.R.	L. Tel.	Rainbow	
Everett R.L.	Ord. Sea.	P.222		Foster B.W.	Sto. 1	Regent	
Eves W.D.H.	S. Lt.	Talisman		Foster C.H.	Era. 3	Umpire	
Eynon M.	Lt. RNVR	H.31		Foster E.	Sto. 1	Shark	
Eyre F.	L. Sea.	Seahorse		Foster G.	L. Sto.	Oxley	
Faber M.E.	Lt.	P.48		Foster G.J.	A.B.	Upholder	MID
Fairclough J.R.	Sto. P.O.	P.615		Foster J.W.T.	P.O.	Spearfish	
Fairfield J.	L. Sea.	Talisman		Foulger J.	Sto. P.O.	Talisman	
Fairholm M.R.	L. Sto.	Phoenix		Foulkes R.J.	A.B.	P.311	
Farbrace P.J.	L. Sea.	Oxley		Foundling W.	Sto. 1	P.311	
Farlow C.	L. Sea.	Stonehenge		Fowell W.A.	Era. 4	Thrasher	
Farlow C.A.J.	A.B.	Phoenix		Fowler H.M.	P.O.	Syrtis	
Farmer R.G.	L. Sto.	Snapper		Fox A.	A.B.	Olympus	
Farnell J.B.	A.B. RNVR	Trooper		Fox A.F.	L. Sea.	Vandal	
Farrington J.P.	Tel.	Rainbow		Fox E.S.S.	A.B.	Orpheus	
Farrington J.R.	Sig.	Tigris		Fox G.	Sto. 1	Sterlet	
Farrow W.E.	L. Sea.	Turbulent		Foxhall P.G.T.	A.B.	Regent	
Faulkner B.	A.B.	Stratagem		Foxon H.R.	Sto. 1	P.311	
Faux F.W.	L. Sea.	Oxley		Frain C.	L. Sea.	Tempest	
Fawkes P.F.	Lt.	Orpheus		Frame F.J.	Ch. Era.	Upholder	DSM
Fazackerley J.	Era. 4	P.33		Frampton K.J.	P.O. Tel.	Grampus	
Fear W.J.	L. Sto.	Salmon		Francis A.R.	C.P.O.	Oxley	
Feary E.W.	P.O.	H.49		Francis C.	Era. 4	Perseus	
Feltham D.A.J.	A.B.	P.311		Francis G.	Wrnt. Engr.	Sickle	
Fenn W.C.E.	Ch. Era.	Trooper	DSM	Francis R.J.	Sto. 1	Simoon	
Fennell A.E.	P.O.	Unique		Frankham J.H.	L. Sto.	Stratagem	
Ferguson A.J.	Tel.	P.38		Franklin H.C.J.	P.O.	Sterlet	
Ferguson J.	A.B.	Tarpon		Frappell L.G.	Sto. 1	Vandal	
Fernie R.R.	S. Lt.	Regent		Fraser A.	Era. 4	H.31	
Fiddes E.H.A.	Sto. P.O.	Tempest		Fraser D.	Sig.	Union	
Fielden W.R.	Wrnt. Engr.	Regulus		Fraser J.N. Mc K.	Elec. Art. 3	Porpoise	
Finlayson A.E.	Sto. P.O.	P.48		Fraser W.	L. Sea.	Rainbow	
Finn J.S.	A.B.	P.222		Freeman F.	A.B.	Splendid	
Finn V.T.	P.O. Tel.	Traveller		Freeman S.	Sto. 1	Talisman	
Firth J.	L. Tel.	Vandal		Freeman S.R.	P.O. Tel.	Thunderbolt	
Fisher F.E.	A.B.	Trooper		Freese J.	Sto. P.O.	Thorn	
Fitall S.C.F.	P.O. Tel.	Unique		Freeth G.G.	Suppy. Asst.	Olympus	
Fleming J.W.	Lt.	Seahorse		French T.W.	Sto. 1	P.311	
Fleming S.	A.B.	Trooper		Frith G.G.W.	Tel.	Unique	
Fleming W.H.	P.O.	Tarpon		Frith R.	Ch. Era.	Unique	
Fletcher T.R.	L. Sea.	Rainbow		Frosr R.S.	Lt. RNR	P.33	
Flinn A.C.	A.B.	Untamed		Frost E.R.	L. Sto.	Odin	
Flockhart P.	Sto. 1	Thorn		Frost P.A.S.	S. Lt.	Usurper	
Florence A.J.	Era. 3	Tigris	DSM	Frost W.J.	Sto. 1	Narwhal	
Flower H.C.	Era. 1	Thames		Fry A.F.	Lt. RNR	Swordfish	
Floyd G.D.	A.B.	Untamed		Fry W.V.	Elec. Art. 3	Trooper	DSM
Flynn D.	P.O.	Talisman	MID	Fuller A.J.	Tel.	Oxley	
Flynn E.J.	P.O. Tel.	Totem		Fuller W.M.	Era. 2	Salmon	
Flynn J.	L. Sto.	Usurper		Furlong J.W.	Elec. Art. 3	Snapper	
Foley J.T.	L. Stwd.	Talisman		Furlong T.E.	Era. 4	P.48	
Forbes G.D.	P.O.	Unbeaten		Furmenger V.A.	A.B.	Undaunted	
Forbes J.H.	Lt. Cmdr.	Spearfish	DSO	Furnell E.C.	A.B.	Trooper	
Ford A.J.	Era. 3	Thames		Furr F.W.	Tel.	Unbeaten	
Ford A.V.	L. Sea.	Triad		Fylan A.P.	A.B.	P.222	
Ford C.D.	A.B.	Turbulent		Fylan J.R.	Sto. P.O.	Usurper	
Ford P.	Y. of S.	Parthian		Fyson D.A.	Lt. RNVR	Syrtis	MID
Foreman C.H.E.	L. Sto.	Orpheus		Gadsby A.C.V.	A.B.	Odin	
Forrester G.W.	L. Sto.	Regulus		Gaffney O.	A.B.	Sirdar	
Forrester W.J.	L. Ck. (s)	Orpheus		Gale E.	A.B.	Unbeaten	
Forsey S.F.	P.O. Ck. (s)	Tigris		Gall C.E.	Sto. 1	Talisman	
Forster L.	L. Sea.	Parthian		Galloway A.F.	L. Tel.	Splendid	
Forster M.	Era. 4	Trooper		Galloway R.M.	Lt.	Union	
Forsyth D.D.	Era. 3	Talisman		Galloway W.T.	A.B.	Thunderbolt	

Name	Rank	Boat	Award
Gambold J.O.	L. Sto.	P.33	
Ganderton R.	L. Sto.	Oxley	
Garbett B.M.	Lt.	Simoon	MID
Gardner G.R.	L. Ck.	Triton	
Gardner T.	P.O. Ck. (s)	Turbulent	DSM
Garfin F.	A.B.	Thistle	
Garland J.	Sto. P.O.	Pandora	
Garner C.E.	Era. 4	Unique	
Garston G.	Sto. 1	Olympus	
Gascoigne A.M.	L. Sea.	Utmost	
Gascoigne W.	A.B.	Porpoise	
Gasser T.J.	Tel.	H.49	
Gates H.J.	L. Sto.	Triumph	
Gates N.J.	L. Sea.	Untamed	
Gathergood J.A.	L. Sto.	Tarpon	
Gatward R.	A.B.	Thistle	
Gauntley S.	A.B.	P.615	
Gavin T.N.	Sto. 1	Turpin	
Geard F.W.J.	Sto. 1	Thames	
Geddes A.	A.B.	Sea Dog	
Gee J.	Sto. 1	P.311	
Gee L.R.	L. Sto.	Regent	
Geeling E.J.	Era. 4	Narwhal	
George A.D.	A.B.	Unbeaten	
Gerrard L.	A.B.	Unbeaten	
Gibbons D.F.	Era. 4	Stratagem	
Gibbons F.B.	A.B.	Thorn	
Gibbs F.B.	Lt.	H.31	
Gibbs J.H.	A.B.	Union	
Gibson A.	A.B.	Porpoise	
Gibson H.	A.B.	Parthian	
Gibson J.J.F.	A.B.	Untamed	
Gibson J.S.	P.O.	Shark	
Gibson P.R.J.	Lt.	Regent	
Gibson W.	A.B.	Parthian	
Gilbert J.B.	P.O.	Trooper	
Gilbert W.A.E.	L. Sea.	Perseus	
Giles A.	Ch. Era.	P.32	
Giles F.A.	Sto. 1	P.222	
Giles F.E.	Sto. 1	Triad	
Gill G.	A.B.	Simoon	
Gill R.V.	Era. 3	Orpheus	
Gillam A.H.	P.O.	Union	
Gillan J.	L. Sea.	P.514	
Gillard S.E.	A.B.	P.222	
Gillespie L.	A.B.	Splendid	
Gillett A.	A.B.	Spearfish	
Gilliam F.	Sto. 1	Parthian	
Gilmore R.	L. Sto.	Sickle	
Gilmour J.	L. Ck. (s)	Tribune	
Gilroy S.	A.B.	Thunderbolt	
Gimblett A.R.	Lt. RNR	Spearfish	
Gissing N.S.	P.O.	Usk	
Glanvill F.	A.B.	Orpheus	
Glanville W.G.	P.O.	Grampus	
Glen J.	Era. 4	Triumph	
Glester W.A.	A.B.	Turbulent	DSM MID
Globe S.	Sto. 1	Tarpon	
Glover A.J.	L. Sea.	Spearfish	
Glover W.H.	A.B.	Turbulent	
Goddard F.G.	P.O. Tel.	Thistle	
Goddard W.J.	Sto. 1	Triumph	
Godtbill P.W.	Sto. 1	Thames	

Name	Rank	Boat	Award
Goffe-Wood W.F.	Sto. 1	H.49	
Golding H.M.	Era. 4	Narwhal	
Golding W.H.	Sto. 1	Thunderbolt	
Goldsmith B.J.	Elec. Art. 4	Syrtis	
Goldsworthy A.	Sto. 2	Turbulent	
Gomer R.C.	P.O. Ck. (s)	Tempest	
Gomm J.E.	Sto. 1	Salmon	
Gooch L.T.	Sto. 1	Triad	
Goodall T.	A.B.	Tarpon	
Goodier J.	Era. 4	Olympus	
Goodman L.T.	L. Sea.	H.31	
Goodman P. D.	Lt. RNVR	Sickle	
Goodwin E.	A.B.	Splendid	
Goodwin H.	A.B.	P.514	
Goodwin J.C.	P.O.	Parthian	
Goodwin J.F.	S. Lt. RNVR	Parthian	
Goodwin K.J.	Sto. 1	Proteus	
Gordon J.H.	Lt. (E)	P.311	
Gorman B.	Tel.	Turbulent	
Gormley F.J.	A.B.	Talisman	
Gosling J.H.	P.O.	Odin	
Goss R.H.	A.B.	Urge	
Gossman D.H.	P.O.	Thorn	
Gough B.	Tel.	Surcouf (Fr.)	
Gough J.	Era. 4	Utmost	
Goulstone F.G.	C.P.O.	P.615	
Gover R.E.	A.B.	P.38	
Govier F.D.	A.B.	Narwhal	
Gowing F.B.	L. Sto.	P.222	
Gowland W.R.	A.B.	Simoon	
Graham J.A.W.	L. Sea.	Rainbow	
Graham R.	Tel.	Stratagem	
Graham W.	Era. 3	Oxley	
Graham W.H.	Tel.	Olympus	
Grainger D.	A.B.	Parthian	
Grainger J.J.	Sto. 2	H.31	
Grant F.C.J.	L. Sea.	Narwhal	
Grant L.A.S.	Lt.	Trooper	DSC
Grant W.J.	Sto. 1	Talisman	
Gratton F.A.J.	A.B.	Swordfish	
Gravell H.	Sto. 1	Union	
Gray A.M.	S. Lt.	P.38	
Gray B.	Civilian War Correspondant	Urge	
Gray J.L.	A.B.	Snapper	
Gray W.R.	L. Sto.	Sterlet	
Greatwood K.N.	A.B.	Trooper	
Greaves C.E.	A.B.	Union	
Greaves C.E.	Era. 2	Phoenix	
Greaves S.M.	L. Sea.	Phoenix	
Green A.M.	Lt.	Regulus	
Green C.C.	A.B.	Sickle	
Green C.S.	Lt.	Narwhal	DSC
Green H.	P.O. Tel.	Parthian	
Green H.A.W.	A.B.	Untamed	
Green H.F.	Tel.	Usk	
Green J.	A.B.	Syrtis	
Greenslade R.H.	Sto. P.O.	Thistle	
Greenway G.H.	Lt. Cmdr.	Tetrarch	
Greenwood S.	Lt. RNR	Clyde	
Gregory A.E.	P.O.	Tarpon	
Gregory C.	Sto. 1	Rainbow	
Gregory E.	Ord. Tel.	Upholder	
Gregory F.W.	Sto. P.O.	Upholder	DSM
Gregory J.F.	L. Tel.	Rainbow	

Gregory P.F.	Sto. 1	Oxley	
Gregson T.W.	L. Sea.	Stratagem	
Greswell B.E.	Lt.	O.13 (Dutch)	
Grey J.W.	Elec. Art. 2	Narwhal	
Griffin J.S.	Era. 4	Perseus	
Griffith B.	P.O.	Simoon	
Griffiths A.E.	A.B.	Porpoise	
Griffiths J.N.	Sto. 2	P.311	
Griffiths P.M.K.	Lt.	Rorqual	
Griffiths S.J.	Sto. 1	P.615	
Griffiths W.J.	Tel.	Usurper	
Groom R.A.	P.O. Tel.	Oxley	
Grounds A.F.	L. Sea.	Sickle	
Grounsell C.T.	A.B.	Regent	
Groves A.L.	A.B.	Traveller	
Groves L.F.	L. Sea.	Urge	
Groves R.R.	Era. 3	Grampus	
Groves W.	Sto. 1	Traveller	BEM
Grubb E.G.	L. Sto.	P.33	
Grummitt A.E.	L. Sea.	Pandora	
Guest G.	L. Sto.	P.38	
Guest W.C.	Ch. Era.	Olympus	
Gumbrell M.W.	Tel.	Olympus	
Gunn R.R.	Sto. 1	P.48	
Gunter R.F.	Sto. 1	Perseus	
Guppy A.N.C.	C.P.O. Tel.	Rainbow	
Gurdy C.S.	Ord. Sea.	P.33	
Guy H.	Era. 2	Triad	
Gynes F.A.J.	P.O. Stwd.	Oxley	
Gyngell J.J.	L. Sea.	Salmon	
Habgood V.A.A.	L. Sig.	Uredd	
Hackett F.G.	A.B.	Regulus	
Haddon F.T.	Tel.	Unbeaten	
Haddon T.R.G.	A.B.	H.44	
Hadfield E.R.	P.O.	Phoenix	
Hadley A.E.	Tel.	Olympus	
Hadley W.K.	C.P.O. Tel.	Turbulent	DSM
Hagan J.	L. Sea.	Tribune	
Hagerty J.P.	Tel.	Syrtis	
Hailey H.L.T.	A.B.	Severn	
Hale A.V.	P.O.	Olympus	
Hale J.W.	L. Tel.	Odin	
Hall A.	A.B.	H.43	
Hall E.	A.B.	Usk	
Hall E.M.	Era. 4	Parthian	
Hall G.A.	A.B.	Tetrarch	
Hall H.J.	L. Sea.	Olympus	
Hall J.D.	Ord. Sea.	Tigris	
Hall K.G.	A.B.	Phoenix	
Hall L.T.	L. Sto.	Thames	
Hall P.E.	A.B.	Salmon	
Hall R.	Elec. Art. 3	Stratagem	
Hall R.	Sto. 1	Turbulent	
Hall W.H.	A.B.	Triumph	MID
Hallett E.E.	A.B.	Sickle	
Halliday I.	A.B.	Grampus	
Halloran D.P.	Wrnt. Engr.	Snapper	
Hallsworth R.S.	A.B.	P.38	
Hallworth J.B.	A.B.	Syrtis	
Hammersley A.F.M.	Elec. Art. 2	Tarpon	
Hammond H.T.	C.P.O.	Thistle	
Hammond N.F.	A.B.	Perseus	
Hammond S. McD. B.	P.O. Tel.	Olympus	
Hancock G.R.	Era. 3	Sickle	

Hancock J.T.	Sig.	O.22 (Dutch)	
Hancock R.H.M.	Lt.	Salmon	DSC
Handy W.	A.B.	Stratagem	
Hankey K.	A.B.	P.33	
Hanna W.J.	A.B.	Phoenix	
Hannah W.S.	Sto. 1	Parthian	
Hannant J.H.	A.B.	Simoon	
Hanson W.	Sto. 1	Parthian	
Harbert H.G.	A.B.	Thames	
Hardacre R.	A.B.	Thistle	
Hardaker G.	C.P.O. Tel.	Orpheus	
Harding V.J.	P.O.	Regent	
Harding W.E.	Sto. 1	Triumph	
Hardwick W.E.	S. Lt. RNVR	Traveller	
Hardy G.F.	Sto. 1	Tempest	
Hardy T.	Era. 3	Triad	
Hardy W.W.	Sto. 1	Stonehenge	
Hare J.S.	L. Sea.	Unity	
Hargreaves E.	L. Sig.	P.32	
Harker J.A.	Sto. 1	Thames	
Harley W.L.G.	Tel.	H.31	
Harman S.G.	Era. 4	Urge	
Harman W.P.	Era. 4	Usurper	
Harms A.J.	Ch. Era.	Undaunted	
Harms J.	A.B.	P.33	
Harnden F.W.	Tel.	Grampus	
Harper K.J.	Lt.	Thistle	
Harratt G.H.	A.B.	Sickle	
Harris C.A.F.	A.B.	Triad	
Harris E.R.	Tel.	Phoenix	
Harris L.G.R.	A.B.	Thames	
Harris N.	A.B.	Spearhead	
Harris V.R.	A.B.	Thunderbolt	
Harris W.	Sto. 1	Simoon	
Harris W.C.	A.B.	Syrtis	
Harrison A.A.G.	Elec. Art. 1	Salmon	
Harrison G.R.H.	A.B.	Triumph	
Harrison P.A.	A.B.	Olympus	
Harrison S.	L. Sea.	Salmon	
Harrison T.C.	A.B.	Tarpon	
Hart A.	C.P.O.	Grampus	
Hart G.A.	A.B.	Tarpon	
Hartland J.	P.O.	Stonehenge	
Hartley A.E.	Stwd.	Perseus	
Hartley J.	Era. 2	Odin	
Hartley W.	Sto. 1	P.222	
Hartshorn G.A.	Ord. Tel.	Undaunted	
Harvey L.J.	L. Tel.	Tarpon	
Harvey R.	A.B.	Regent	
Haselfoot W.F.	Lt. Cmdr.	Thistle	
Hastie J.	Sto. 1	Undaunted	
Hatchard A.J.	P.O.	Thorn	
Hatton C.W.	A.B.	Simoon	
Haward G.H.S.	Lt. Cmdr.	Sterlet	
Hawes E.H.D.	A.B.	Spearfish	
Hawkins A.H.	Sto. 1	Orpheus	
Hawkyard D.	S. Lt. RNR	P.39	
Hay G.	Sto. 1	Turbulent	
Hayburn A.J.	A.B.	Talisman	
Haydon H.S.	Sto. 1	Talisman	
Hayes F.G.	Sto. 1	P.615	
Hayes J.	A.B.	Stratagem	
Hayes P.	Ch. Sto.	Thorn	
Hayler C.L.	Ord. Sea.	Thorn	

Name	Rank	Ship	Award
Hayter R.H.	L. Sto.	Union	
Hayward A.E.	Ch. Era.	Triad	MID
Hayward H.J.	L. Sto.	Rainbow	
Hayward L.E.	L. Tel.	Thorn	
Haywood F.C.	Sto. 1	Parthian	
Hazzard K.	Sto. 1	Talisman	
Heal H.V.	Sto. 1	Undaunted	
Healey A.	Sto. P.O.	Porpoise	
Healey M.W.	L. Sea.	Thistle	
Healey W.W.	L. Tel.	Thistle	
Heard H.	L. Ck.	Tetrarch	
Hearn A.E.	P.O. Stwd.	Narwhal	
Hearnden W.H.	P.O.	Tetrarch	MID
Heath A.T.	L. Sto.	Upholder	
Heathcote E.	L. Sea.	Thunderbolt	
Heaton J.	A.B.	Parthian	
Hedges P.	A.B.	Traveller	
Hedley W.	Sto. P.O.	Grampus	
Heenan T.M.H.	A.B.	Parthian	
Hellyer R.	Era. 2	Urge	
Hemelryk A.	Lt.	P.222	
Hemingway R.J.	Lt.	P.38	
Henden F.W.H.	P.O.	Thorn	
Henderson A.	Era. 4	Porpoise	
Henderson C.	A.B.	Perseus	
Henderson G.J.	A.B.	Oxley	
Henderson G.M.	Era. 3	Narwhal	
Henderson M.G.	Lt.	Phoenix	
Hendy W.G.R.	L. Sto.	Narwhal	
Henshall G.	L. Sea.	Syrtis	
Henson H.W.	Tel.	Umpire	
Henson L.	L. Sto.	Porpoise	
Hepworth E.	L. Sto.	Tetrarch	
Herbert D.V.	Tel.	P.222	
Herbert L.W.	Sto. 1	Splendid	
Herd C.E.	Ord. Sea.	Simoon	
Herrett D.	Sto. 1	H.49	
Herstell N.	A.B.	Simoon	
Heseltine R.J.	A.B.	Pandora	
Heselton J.	L. Ck.	Grampus	
Hetherington R.	A.B.	Parthian	
Hewett J.P.	L. Tel.	Thames	
Hewitt A.	A.B.	Regent	
Hewlett F.	Sto. 1	Traveller	
Heywood R.	A.B.	P.48	
Hibbert J.G.	Tel.	Saracen	
Hickey C.A.	P.O. Ck. (s)	Oxley	
Hickley J.H.	S. Lt. RNVR	Vandal	
Hickman F.J.	Wrnt. Engr.	Pandora	DSC
Hickman J.G.	Sto. 1	Clyde	
Hickson W.	A.B.	Untamed	
Higdon R.T.	A.B.	Phoenix	
Higgins A.G.	Sto. 1	Phoenix	
Higgins G.T.C.	S. Lt. RNVR	Untamed	
Higgs J.W.	Ord. Sea.	Vandal	
Highmore J.W.	P.O.	Olympus	
Hill B.D.	A.B.	Parthian	
Hill J.A.	A.B.	Tigris	
Hill N.J.	Ch. Era.	Salmon	
Hill P.N.B.L.	A.B.	Olympus	
Hill R.E.	A.B.	Spearfish	
Hill R.H.	L. Sto.	Syrtis	
Hill W.E.H.	Sto. 1	Snapper	
Hillcoat T.M.	Sto. 1	Undaunted	
Hills A.A.	A.B.	Tarpon	
Hills F.G.	L. Sig.	H.49	
Hills H.C.	A.B.	Traveller	
Hillyard H.	Era. 3	P.319	
Hilton J.H.	Sto. 1	Usurper	
Hind G.M.	A.B.	Trooper	
Hinde H.J.	C.P.O.	Triton	DSM
Hinds A.C.	C.P.O.	Vandal	DSM
Hinds J.	L. Sea.	Triumph	
Hindson J.	Sto. 1	Thames	
Hines R.H.	Sto. 1	Seahorse	
Hines V.W.	L. Sto.	Thunderbolt	
Hirst L.	L. Sto.	Stonehenge	
Hiscock W.J.	Ch. Era.	Porpoise	DSM
Hitchcock R.D.	Era. 4	Pandora	
Hitchcock R.G.	Elec. Art. 2	Regulus	
Hitchcock T.J.	L. Tel.	Regent	
Hoath J.S.	Sto. 1	Olympus	
Hobbs H.T.B.	A.B.	H.49	
Hobbs R.A.	L. Tel.	Snapper	
Hockless G.W.	A.B.	Sickle	
Hodge R.E.	A.B.	Grampus	
Hodgkinson R.L.	A.B.	Utmost	
Hodgkinson S.	A.B.	Stonehenge	
Hodson H.	Era. 3	Rainbow	
Hodson R.E.	Sto. 1	Perseus	
Hodson W.	Sto. 1	Splendid	
Hoey P.J.	L. Sea.	Umpire	
Hogben G.H.	Sto. P.O.	Pandora	
Hogg W.	P.O.	Turbulent	
Hoggett H.J.R.	Ch. Era.	Tarpon	
Holden J.W.	Tel.	Perseus	
Holder F.	Sto. 1	Syrtis	
Holland B.	Era. 4	Stonehenge	
Holland G.H.	A.B.	Unique	
Holland G.W.	L. Sea.	Spearfish	
Holliday W.	L. Stwd.	Tarpon	
Hollingworth A.C.	L. Sea.	Swordfish	
Hollingworth G.A.	P.O.	Phoenix	
Holman A.R.	Era. 4	Traveller	
Holman B.J.	L. Sea.	Odin	
Holman H.	Sto. 1	Parthian	
Holmes C.W.	P.O.	Salmon	
Holroyd N.	Sto. 1	Rainbow	
Holroyd W.	L. Sto.	H.31	
Holt F.	A.B.	P.514	
Holt F.H.	A.B.	Olympus	
Holt H.	Sto. 1	Oxley	
Holt W.	Sto. 1	Saracen	
Honeysett F.R.J.	Tel.	P.32	
Hood A.G.	A.B.	Porpoise	
Hooper F.A.	Sto. 1	Stonehenge	
Hooton W.H.	A.B.	Traveller	
Hopcroft T.G.	A.B.	Regulus	
Hopkins W.J.	A.B.	Oxley	
Horick G.P.	Lt.	Thunderbolt	
Hornsby E.	P.O. Tel.	Tetrarch	
Horstead A.A.	L. Sea.	Narwhal	
Horton H.G.	L. Sto.	Trooper	
Horton R.	Sto. 1	Triad	
Horton W.R.	L. Sea.	Regent	
Horwood E.S.	Era. 2	Regulus	
Hosie A.	L. Ck. (s)	Syrtis	
Houston R.B.	S. Lt.	Tetrarch	

Houston W.J.	Sto. 1	Umpire	
Howard A.	Elec. Art. 2	Thistle	
Howard F.A.	A.B.	Stonehenge	
Howard G.H.	P.O.	Stratagem	
Howard J.E.	L. Sea.	P.48	
Howard R.	L. Sea.	Triumph	
Howard W.B.	A.B.	Thames	
Howe E.H.	A.B.	Salmon	
Howell N.L.E.	Era. 3	Phoenix	
Howell R.	Sto. 1	Regent	
Howells D.J.	Sto. 1	Triad	
Howes H.G.	Wrnt. Engr.	Olympus	
Howes R.E.N.	S. Lt.	Stonehenge	
Howlett G.L.	P.O.	P.33	
Hubbard C.C.	P.O.	P.615	
Hubbard F.P.D.	A.B.	Tarpon	
Hubbard W.F.	Era. 4	Traveller	
Huddart J.S.	Lt.	Triumph	
Hudson J.K.	L. Sto.	Regent	
Huelin G.J.	L. Sea.	Narwhal	MID
Hughes C.W.T.	Sto. 1	Porpoise	
Hughes F.	Sig.	Sterlet	
Hughes G.	A.B.	Upholder	MID
Hughes J.A.	L. Sto.	Pandora	
Hughes J.K.	A.B.	Thunderbolt	
Hulbert W.B.	Lt.	Traveller	
Hull J.	Tel.	H.49	
Hull L.	L. Sto.	Syrtis	
Hull W.	Era. 3	Perseus	
Hume T.W.	A.B.	Triad	
Humphrey J.E.	L. Sea.	Phoenix	
Hunnisett B.	A.B.	Turbulent	
Hunt E.G.	Era. 4	P.311	
Hunter L.	L. Sto.	Odin	
Hunter R.	Sto. 1	Traveller	
Hunter W.G.	Sto. 1	Oxley	
Hurley J.B.	A.B.	H.31	
Hurlock A.E.	A.B.	Olympus	
Hurst P.	L. Sea.	Tigris	
Hussey W.S.	L. Sto.	Thistle	
Hussey-Yeo L.D.	A.B.	Thunderbolt	
Hutchings J.J.	Tel.	Traveller	
Hutchinson D.G.	L. Sea.	Triumph	DSM
Hutchison J.	A.B.	Vandal	
Hutton N.W.	L. Sea.	Traveller	
Hyde C.E.	Sto. 1	Tigris	
Hyde J.H.	Sto. 1	Seahorse	
I'anson J.H.	Era. 3	Thistle	
Ibbotson W.	C.P.O.	Spearfish	
Iddiolis C.	P.O.	P.311	
Imison D.H.	L. Sto.	Regent	
Imrie D.	A.B.	Parthian	
Incledon L.J.	S. Lt.	Thorn	
Ingram F.G.	L. Sea.	P.48	
Ingram J.M.F.	Sto. 1	Triad	
Irvine D.	Sto. 1	Thames	
Isaac D.J.	Era. 1	Undaunted	
Iverson W.S.	L. Sea.	Spearfish	
Jack T.	L. Sea.	Sickle	
Jackman C.J.	C.P.O.	Urge	DSM*
Jackman J.A.	L. Sto.	Olympus	DSM
Jackson C.T.	L. Tel.	Triton	
Jackson J.W.	Sto. 1	Oxley	
Jackson L.P.	A.B.	Usurper	
Jackson M.R.	S. Lt.	O.22 (Dutch)	
Jackson P.G.W.	Tel.	Tempest	
Jackson R.	Elec. Art. 3	Talisman	DSM
Jackson W.	Sto. 2	P.38	
Jacob L.C.N.	Era. 4	Parthian	
Jacobs A.R.	Sto. 1	Tetrarch	
Jacobs L.D.	P.O. Tel.	Vandal	
Jacques H.S.	P.O. Tel.	Sterlet	
Jago T.E.	L. Sig.	P.33	
Jakeman P.B.	Lt. RNVR	Sickle	
Jakins T.	Sto. 1	Vandal	
James A.E.	L. Sea.	Phoenix	
James F.S.	A.B.	Talisman	
James R.A.	A.B. RNVR	Upholder	
James R.S.	L. Sto.	P.514	
James T.B.	A.B.	Spearfish	
James W.	A.B.	P.615	
James W.D.	A.B.	P.614	
Jamieson W.	Era. 4	Syrtis	
Jancy S.	L. Sea.	Talisman	
Janvrin M.C.	Lt.	Triumph	DSC MID
Japp A.W.	Tel.	Thunderbolt	
Jarvis A.H.	P.O.	Narwhal	
Jarvis E.N.	Ch. Era.	H.31	
Jarvis R.W.	A.B.	Olympus	
Jeffery J.	Sig.	Rainbow	
Jehu T.L.	A.B.	P.33	
Jenkins H.L.	Sto. 1	Oxley	
Jenkinson J.W.	Tel.	Seahorse	
Jenner H.	Ch. Era.	P.37	
Jennings H.	L. Sig.	Umpire	
Jennings T.C.	Sto. 1	Tetrarch	
John W.M.	Tel.	P.48	
Johns R.W.	A.B.	P.311	
Johns T.G.	Elec. Art. 2	Odin	
Johns W.H.	Era. 4	Narwhal	
Johnson A.	Wrnt. Engr.	Perseus	
Johnson F.	Sto. P.O.	Regulus	
Johnson F.W.	C.P.O.	Triad	
Johnson R.J.	A.B.	Simoon	
Johnson S.L.	A.B.	Thunderbolt	
Johnston A.H.	Sto. 1	Thames	
Johnstone W.P.D.	P.O.	Usurper	
Jones A.H.	Era. 4	Regent	
Jones C.	A.B.	Perseus	
Jones C.E.	Sto. P.O.	Vandal	
Jones E.B.	L. Sig.	Usk	
Jones E.L.	A.B.	Swordfish	
Jones E.T.	A.B.	Parthian	
Jones F.H.	A.B.	P.222	
Jones F.R.	A.B.	Olympus	
Jones H.F.	A.B.	Sterlet	
Jones J.	A.B.	Thorn	
Jones J.	Sto. 1	Parthian	
Jones J.F.	L. Tel.	Triton	
Jones J.H.G.	L. Sea.	Triad	
Jones K.A.E.	L. Stwd.	Olympus	
Jones K.W.	Era. 3	Snapper	
Jones L.	Era. 4	Sickle	
Jones L.	A.B.	Triumph	MID
Jones L.A.	Lt.	Thistle	
Jones L.F.	S. Lt. RNVR	Simoon	
Jones L.W.	Ord. Sea.	Tetrarch	

Jones N.C.	Sig.	H.31	
Jones N.E.	A.B.	Turbulent	
Jones R.	A.B.	Trooper	
Jones R.W.C.	P.O. Tel.	Satyr	
Jones S.	Sto. 2	Parthian	
Jones S.B.	A.B.	Utmost	
Jones S.F.	P.O.	Regulus	
Jones T.B.	L. Tel.	Pandora	
Jones W.C.	Sto. P.O.	Orpheus	
Jonsson A.F.F.	A.B.	Triad	
Jope W.P.	Sto. 1	Tarpon	
Jordan G.A.	A.B.	Usk	
Jordan M.	Sto. 1	Oxley	
Jordan S.L.	Lt.	Usurper	
Joss R.F.	Era. 3	Thistle	
Julian R.E.B.	A.B.	Porpoise	
Jupp M.H.	Lt.	Syrtis	DSC
Jury A.E.	L. Sto.	Tempest	MID
Kane F.	Sto. 1	Thames	
Kavanagh S.W.	Sto. 1	Odin	
Kay F.	L. Sto.	Sterlet	
Kay J.M.	Ord. Sea.	Syrtis	
Keary F.A.	L. Sto.	Perseus	
Keefe C.R.	Sig.	Una	
Keenan P.	P.O. Ck. (s)	Parthian	
Keenan R.	A.B.	Thunderbolt	
Keers J.	Sto. 2	Union	
Keith-Roach M.	Lt.	Triad	DSC
Kellaway H.S.	Sto. 1	Usk	
Kellaway L.R.	A.B.	Orpheus	
Kellet O.	P.O.	Swordfish	
Kellond R.	Era. 2	Tarpon	
Kelly C.	L. Sto.	Triumph	
Kelly D.	Sto. 1	Tempest	
Kelly P.	Sto. 1	P.32	
Kelsey R.	A.B.	Thunderbolt	
Kemp W.H.	L. Sto.	Orpheus	
Kempshall R.A.	L. Sto.	Union	
Kempthorne L.R.	A.B.	Splendid	
Kennard V.A.	Sto. P.O.	Swordfish	
Kennedy G.A.	L. Tel.	Simoon	
Kennedy M.H.McL	Lt.	Porpoise	
Kennett D.F.	A.B.	Tetrarch	
Kent-Smith P.J.	Era. 4	P.615	
Kerr D.A.	Era. 4	Simoon	
Kerr R.C.	Ch. Era.	Odin	
Kerr W.T.	Sto. P.O.	P.38	
Kerry A.	P.O. Tel.	P.222	
Kerry D.J.	Tel.	Tetrarch	
erry L.L.	L. Tel.	Porpoise	
Kettle C.	L. Sto.	Utmost	DSM
ettle L.H.	Lt.	Tarpon	
Kewell J.R.	L. Sto.	Seahorse	
ey A.	A.B.	P.311	
eyte J.P.	A.B.	P.48	
eyzar H.F.	Ch. Era.	Thames	
ilty T.J.	L. Sig.	Triumph	
imberley C.	Ch. Era.	P.311	
ing A.G.	L. Sig.	Regulus	
ing C.W.	P.O. Tel.	Undaunted	
ing J.C.	P.O. Stwd.	P.311	MID
ing J.T.	Sto. 1	Triton	
ing R.F.	L. Sto.	Perseus	
ing R.G.	A.B.	Regent	
King R.H.	Elec. Art. 4	Stonehenge	
King R.S.	L. Sig.	Thunderbolt	
King W.E.	P.O.	Tigris	
Kirby M.W.	L. Sto.	Talisman	
Kirby N.V.	L. Sig.	Regulus	
Kirby W.E.	L. Tel.	Regulus	
Kirton J.P.	Ck. (s)	Pandora	
Kirwin K.J.	C.P.O.	Stonehenge	
Kissane J.C.	P.O. Ck. (s)	Stonehenge	
Kitching H.C.	Sto. 1	Narwhal	
Kitson J.	Elec. Art. 1	Orpheus	
Knott A.E.	A.B.	Olympus	
Knowles A.C.	L. Sig.	H.49	
Knowles M.H.	Sto. 2	Usurper	
Knox W.J.	A.B.	P.222	
Knox W.N.R.	Lt.	Regent	DSC
Laing G.	A.B.	P.514	
Laird J.B.	A.B.	Thorn	
Laister G.	L. Sea.	Olympus	
Lake E.C.	P.O.	Sterlet	
Laker J.W.	C.P.O.	Snapper	
Lamb J.W.	L. Sto.	Urge	
Lambert C.W. StC.	Lt.	P.615	DSC*
Lancaster F.A.	L. Sea.	Triumph	
Lancaster H.	A.B.	Sterlet	
Lancaster O.F.	Lt. (E)	Trooper	DSC
Landers E.W.	L. Tel.	Oxley	
Landing J.	L. Sto.	Simoon	
Lane S.F.	A.B.	Upholder	
Lang A.	Sto. 1	Triton	
Langford A.J.	P.O.	Otus	
Langley M.A.	Lt.	Swordfish	DSC
Langridge A.O.	Sto. P.O.	Sterlet	
Lattimore S.G.	Sto. P.O.	Perseus	
Laurance J.S.	Ch. Era.	Unbeaten	DSM
Lavender F.	Sto. 1	Tempest	
Lavers E.J.B.	Era. 3	Triton	
Lavery W.M.	A.B.	Salmon	
Law A.S.	Sto. 2	Perseus	
Law E.C.	L. Sig.	Urge	MID
Law N.	Sto. P.O.	Olympus	
Lawler P.J.A.	A.B.	P.38	
Lawrence D.	P.O.	Splendid	
Lawrenson D.R.	Era. 4	Seahorse	
Laws W.G.	L. Sea.	Odin	
Lawson A.L.J.	L. Sto.	P.48	
Lawson C.C.	L. Sto.	Trooper	
Lawson G.	Sto. 1	Narwhal	
Lawson J.M.	S. Lt.	Turbulent	
Lawson M.E.	L. Sea.	Snapper	
Lea R.H.	Era. 4	Tigris	
Leader E.	Era. 4	Odin	
Leaf S.J.	Era. 4	Unbeaten	DSM
Learmouth D.H.	Era. 4	Sickle	
Leathy W.H.	A.B.	Odin	
Lee A.E.H.	P.O.	Utmost	
Lee A.S.K.	C.P.O.	P.311	DSM
Lee C.T.G.	L. Ck. (s)	Sickle	
Lee G.	P.O.	Stratagem	
Lee J.A.	P.O.	Thunderbolt	
Lee J.E.	Era. 3	Thames	
Lee P.L.C.M.	S. Lt.	Odin	
Lee P.S.	Sto. P.O.	Seahorse	
Lee R.D.	L. Sea.	Regent	

Lee W.T.	Era. 2	Swordfish	
Leech A.J.	L. Sea.	Regulus	
Leech H.	Sto. P.O.	Regent	
Leeke R.W.	L. Sig.	Urge	
Lees H.	Era. 4	Tigris	MID
Legassick W.	Sig.	Splendid	
Legg A.F.	L. Sto.	Trooper	
Legg R.	Sto. 2	Pandora	
Leggatt D.W.	Lt.	Usk	
Lehane F.	L. Sto.	Perseus	
Leigh L.	Sto. 1	Olympus	
Lemin J.	Sto. P.O.	Regent	
Lennox J.	A.B.	Utmost	
Leonard F.	L. Sea.	Phoenix	
Leonard W.	L. Sto.	Tarpon	
Lethbridge R.P.	Tel.	Olympus	
Lever R.B.	L. Sto.	Utmost	
Lewer J.M.	Era. 3	Undaunted	
Lewin A.C.	L. Sto.	Pandora	
Lewin W.W.	Sto. 1	Umpire	
Lewis A.E.	Era. 4	Talisman	
Lewis C.H.	A.B.	Union	
Lickiss G.L.	L. Tel.	Tetrarch	
Liddle F.	L. Sto.	Triton	
Lidstone A.E.	Ord. Sea.	P.514	
Lightfoot F.	P.O.	Parthian	
Lillford C.	L. Sto.	Perseus	
Lillycrop F.W.	Sto. 1	Simoon	
Lincoln W.G.	Elec. Art.	Tigris	DSM
Lindsell J.A.	Lt.	Olympus	
Linton J.W.	Cmdr.	Turbulent	VC DSO DSC
Lipscombe L.A.	A.B.	Regent	
Little A.	Era. 4	Usurper	
Liversidge G.A.	Lt.	Phoenix	
Livesay H.	L. Sto.	Oxley	
Livesey C.J.	L. Sea.	Thistle	
Livesley J.L.	Lt.	Undaunted	
Livingston A.	L. Sto.	Porpoise	
Livingstone G.R.	P.O. Tel.	Tetrarch	MID
Lloyd A.M.	A.B.	Perseus	
Lloyd C.A.	Sto. P.O.	Turbulent	MID
Lloyd H.R.	A.B.	Trooper	
Lloyd R.W.	Sto. 1	Regent	
Lloyd S.A.	L. Sto.	Sterlet	
Lock G.L.	Sto. 1	Tigris	
Lockwood A.F.	A.B.	Union	
Lockwood W.F.	A.B.	Undaunted	
Loines C.W.L.	Ord. Sea.	Swordfish	
Lomas R.	Ch. Era.	Oxley	
Long S.H.	Tel.	Grampus	
Loose D.E.A.	Era. 4	Tempest	
Lord G.	A.B.	P.311	
Lord J.	L. Tel.	P.311	
Loughran H.	Sto. 1	Regent	
Lound R.C.	Sto. 1	Oxley	
Lovell E.A.	A.B.	Simoon	
Low J.N.A.	Lt.	Unity	
Lowe F.	Sto. P.O.	Thunderbolt	
Lowe W.A.	L. Sto.	Stonehenge	MID
Lowery A.	A.B.	P.615	
Lowin E.T.J.	L. Sea.	Tempest	
Lowis R.E.	P.O.	Regent	
Loxley R.	A.B.	Odin	

Lucas H.G.	L. Sto.	Tetrarch	
Luckham H.J.	Ord. Sea.	Perseus	
Lucking C.J.	L. Sto.	Porpoise	
Luff R.	Sto. 1	Tarpon	
Luker J.W.	Tel.	Thistle	
Lumby R.	Sto. 1	Orpheus	
Lyfield A.R.	C.P.O.	Turbulent	MID
Lynch D.H.	Wrnt. Engr.	Syrtis	DSM
Lynch F.	A.B.	Spearfish	
Lynch J.F.	P.O. Tel.	Pandora	
Lynch R.	Ch. Era.	Thunderbolt	
Lyons T.	Tel.	P.32	
Lyth J.L.	Elec. Art. 4	P.311	
Mace A.E.	L. Sto.	Odin	
MacIntosh A.F.	A.B.	Supreme	
Mack D.W.	P.O. Ck. (s)	Talisman	
Mack F.C.H.	Tel.	Regulus	
Mackay D.J.	A.B.	Sickle	
Macken T.	Sto. 1	Splendid	
Mackenzie A.J.	Lt. Cmdr.	P.222	
MacKenzie D.	C.P.O.	Syrtis	
MacLeod D.A.	Sto. 1	Thunderbolt	
Macrae I.N.	Lt.	P.311	
Maddison G.E.	Sto. 1	Thistle	
Magness W.S.	P.O.	Thorn	MID
Mahoney P.	A.B.	Talisman	
Maidment J.	L. Tel.	Urge	
Malcolm J.	A.B.	Unbeaten	
Male P.	Ord. Sea.	Untamed	
Mallett R.G.	L. Tel.	Salmon	
Malley L.	Sto. P.O.	Syrtis	
Malliband G.G.	Sto. 1	Porpoise	
Manley F.K.	Lt. RNR	Oxley	
Mann D.A.W.G.	P.O.	Regulus	
Manson A.	A.B.	P.222	
Manton T.	Sto. 1	Regulus	
Manuel W.J.	P.O.	Orpheus	
Maples C.	L. Tel.	Thorn	
Mapplebeck P.	A.B.	P.311	
Mapstone A.A.B.	A.B.	Perseus	
Marchant W.C.	L. Tel.	Narwhal	MID
Marchant W.H.	L. Tel.	Olympus	
Marner J.H.	L. Sea.	Thames	
Marriott N.	Lt.	P.39	DSC
Marriott P.A.	Sto. 1	Grampus	
Marsden H.	Sto. 1	Narwhal	
Marsden T.	Era. 4	Simoon	
Marsh L.	Sto. 1	Pandora	
Marshall A.R.	Sto. 2	Talisman	
Marshall J.E.	Sto. 1	Seahorse	
Marshall R.	A.B.	Sickle	
Marshall W.A.	Era. 3	Grampus	
Martin A.H.	Lt.	Unique	
Martin B.H.	P.O.	Porpoise	
Martin F.A.	Era. 2	Union	
Martin F.J.	P.O.	Upholder	
Martin G.	Sto. P.O.	Stonehenge	
Martin G.G.	P.O.	Orpheus	
Martin G.J.	Sto. 1	Sterlet	
Martin J.H.	Sto. P.O.	Oxley	
Martin R.C.W.	Era. 4	P.311	
Martin S.	L. Sto.	Sickle	
Martin S.	Tel.	Olympus	
Martin S.J.	Tel.	Tetrarch	

Name	Rank	Boat	Award
Martin W.H.	Era. 2	P.32	
Martin W.J.A.J.	Era. 3	Usk	
Mason G.H.	L. Sto.	Simoon	
Mason G.L.	Era. 4	Turbulent	
Mason G.R.	A.B.	P.514	
Massy-Dawson D.S.	Lt.	Seahorse	
Mather J.	Era. 4	Trooper	
Mathews G.F.	Sto. 1	Regent	
Matthews E.G.	P.O.	Snapper	MID
Matthews F.W.	Ord. Sea.	Triton	
Matthews R.	Sto. 1	Phoenix	
Maw E.P.	Lt. RNVR	Thunderbolt	
Mawson L.	A.B.	H.34	
Maxwell M.J.	Sto. 1	Spearfish	
May S.J.	A.B.	Simoon	
Maynard A.E.	A.B.	H.31	
Maynard A.E.	Sto. 1	Turbulent	
Mayne R.C.	A.B.	Seahorse	
McAlinden F.J.	L. Sea.	Stratagem	
McAlister J.	P.O.	P.514	
McAllister W.	L. Sto.	Syrtis	
McAteer R.B.P.	P.O. Ck. (s)	Regulus	
McBeth J.D.	L. Sto.	P.48	
McBride J.N.	P.O.	Tetrarch	MID
McBride W.	Tel.	Traveller	
McCabe J.	A.B.	Parthian	
McCaig J.V.	L. Stwd.	Parthian	
McCarron J.A.P.	A.B.	Tigris	
McCarthy D.	Sto. 1	Thorn	
McCarthy R.D.	Sig.	Syrtis	
McCauley T.	Sto. P.O.	Stratagem	
McCleave T.J.	Sto. 2	Snapper	
McClinton R.W.	L. Tel.	P.615	
McClure J.	P.O. Tel.	Regulus	
McCombe R.B.	Sto. P.O.	P.311	
McConville P.E.	L. Sto.	Grampus	
McDiarmid F.	A.B.	Urge	
McDonald D.	A.B.	Perseus	
McDonald H.P.	L. Tel.	O.13 (Dutch)	
McDowall J.R.	L. Sto.	P.514	
McEdward J.C.	A.B.	Talisman	
McGee W.	Sto. 1	Triumph	
McGhee E.	L. Sto.	Regulus	
McGow E.	Sto. 1	Thunderbolt	
McGrath M.	A.B.	Orpheus	
McGuigan E.J.	A.B.	P.615	
McGuire J.	Sto. P.O.	Traveller	
McInnes C.	Era. 4	Thorn	
McIntosh A.F.	A.B.	P.48	
McKay S.N.	A.B.	H.49	
McKay W.	Ch. Era.	Stratagem	
McKinstry C.	Sto. P.O.	Rainbow	
McLachlan J.	A.B.	Utmost	
McLane W.	Ord. Sea.	P.32	
McLaren W.	L. Sea.	P.48	
McLaughlan J.	L. Sea.	P.615	
McLean A.W.	L. Sto.	Orpheus	
McLean W.	Ord. Sea.	P.311	
McLennan H.B.W.	L. Tel.	Simoon	
McLeod D.M.	A.B.	P.314	
McLoughlin N.	Sto. 1	Orpheus	
McMahon C.			
McMahon J.	L. Tel.	P.33	
McMann T.	L. Tel.	Swordfish	
McMillan A.	P.O.	Rainbow	
McMillan J.C.D.	Sto. 1	Urge	
McMilling J.A.	L. Sea.	Regulus	
McNally D.	Sto. 1	Thunderbolt	
McNally J.E.	L. Sto.	Orpheus	
McNally W.J.	Commd. Engr.	Talisman	
McNeilage C.	Sto. P.O.	P.33	
McNeill W.B.	A.B.	Sickle	
McShane T.N.	Sto. 1	P.311	
Mead C.E.	A.B.	Perseus	
Mead J.B.	A.B.	Unique	
Meaker E.K.	A.B.	Usurper	
Mealyou A.R.	A.B.	P.48	
Mechen W.T.	Sto. 2	Pandora	
Medley J.	Sto. 1	P.33	
Meek F.H.	Sto. 1	Trooper	
Meek J.A.	A.B.	Tempest	
Meek R.C.F.	P.O.	Perseus	
Meikle A.	A.B.	Traveller	
Melhuish R.T.W.	A.B.	P.48	
Mellows G.H.	A.B.	Snapper	
Menzies C.J.	A.B.	Vandal	
Mercer C.A.G.	L. Tel.	P.38	
Mercer N.W.	Era. 3	Sterlet	
Mercer S.	Stwd.	Trooper	
Meredith T.	Sto. 1	Utmost	
Merkel P.T.	P.O.	P.38	
Merritt A.I.	Lt.	H.31	
Merritt R.J.	A.B.	Talisman	
Messenger F.P.	P.O.	Grampus	
Metherell G.H.	A.B.	P.311	
Meyrick K.W.M.	Lt.	Tetrarch	
Micklefield F.	L. Sto.	Undaunted	
Milburn J.J.	Sto. 1	Thorn	
Miles F.A.	L. Sto.	Untamed	
Milford J.R.	Sto. 1	P.514	
Millar M.F.	S. Lt.	P.32	
Miller C.	L. Sto.	Oxley	
Miller D.A.	P.O.	Upholder	DSM*
Miller E.F.	A.B.	Vandal	
Miller H.J.	A.B.	Unity	
Miller W.C.E.	L. Tel.	Odin	
Millerick F.F.	Sto. 1	Swordfish	
Milligan J.T.	A.B.	Talisman	
Milligan J.V.	Sto. P.O.	P.311	
Milliken T.E.	P.O. Stwd.	Thorn	
Mills E.P.	Sto. 1	Traveller	
Mills R.W.	L. Sto.	Trooper	
Millson R.V.	A.B.	Thames	
Millward P.R.	Sto. 1	Tudor	
Milne R.G.	Wrnt. Engr.	Triton	DSC
Milner G.D.N.	Lt.	Simoon	DSC
Milne-Thomson P.R.A.	Lt.	Olympus	
Mingay A.G.	P.O.	Oxley	
Mitchell B.H.	A.B.	Stratagem	
Mitchell C.J.	C.P.O.	Sickle	
Mitchell C.R.	Elec. Art. 1	Oxley	
Mitchell J.H.	L. Tel.	Regulus	
Mitchell L.C.	Tel.	Untamed	
Mitchell R.E.	A.B.	Thunderbolt	
Mitchell R.G.	Era. 2	Narwhal	
Mitchell T.	A.B.	Thorn	
Mitchell W.E.	Era. 1	Thistle	
Mitton L.H.	L. Sig.	Unbeaten	

Name	Rank	Boat	Award
Mobbs S.N.	L. Sea.	Sickle	
Mockett J.	Era. 3	Oxley	
Molesworth C.A.	A.B.	Tetrarch	
Molloy C.A.	Era. 4	Stonehenge	
Moncrieff R. McC.	L. Sea.	Traveller	
Montador J.	Sto. 1	Narval (Fr.)	
Moody E.R.	A.B.	Thames	
Moody J.	A.B.	Splendid	
Moon T.H.	Y. of S.	P.311	
Moon W.H.	L. Sto.	Tigris	MID
Moor J.	A.B.	Narwhal	
Moorcroft R.G.	Era. 3	Thorn	
Moore C.H.	L. Sto.	Triton	
Moore L.J.	A.B.	Thunderbolt	DSM
Moore L.P.	Lt. Cmdr.	Rainbow	
Moores A.	L. Sto.	Regent	
Moorhouse T.	L. Sea.	Stratagem	
Morcomb T.	Sto. 1	P.33	
Mordue J.	Sto. 1	Spearfish	
Morel E.P.C.	L. Sea.	Narval (Fr.)	
Moreton C.W.	A.B.	Union	
Morey E.G.	A.B.	Spearfish	DSM MID
Morgan A.B.	L. Sea.	Seahorse	
Morgan J.	A.B.	Triton	
Morgan J.E.W.	P.O.	P.222	
Morgan J.L.	L. Sto.	Thistle	
Morgan P.	P.O.	Triad	
Morgan W.D.	A.B.	Unbeaten	
Morley G.E.	A.B.	Unbeaten	
Morris C.B.	Tel.	P.33	
Morris C.E.	A.B.	Turbulent	
Morris E.	P.O.	Talisman	
Morris F.C.	Elec. Art. 1	Turbulent	DSM
Morris F.E.J.	L. Tel.	Triad	
Morris F.H.	L. Sea.	Urge	
Morris F.H.	Lt.	Thames	
Morris R.H.	L. Sto.	Oxley	
Morris R.L.S.	Lt.	P.32	
Morris W.R.	L. Sea.	Odin	
Morrison C.A.	L. Sto.	Swordfish	
Morrison G.E.	A.B.	Undaunted	
Morrison J.	Sto. 1	Tempest	
Morrison K.	A.B.	Tetrarch	
Morrison W.	A.B.	P.33	
Morrow T.A.D.	P.O.	Traveller	MID
Morse R.F.	Ord. Sig.	H.31	
Morse W.G.	A.B.	Talisman	DSM
Morten M.F.	A.B.	Unique	
Mortimer-Lamb R.J.	P.O.	Simoon	
Morton J.	L. Sea.	Talent	
Morton J.R.	L. Sto.	P.222	
Morton R.J.	Sto. 1	Regulus	
Morton T.W.	L. Sto.	Phoenix	
Moss E.	L. Sto.	Unique	
Moss S.	Era. 4	Vandal	
Mott D.R.O.	Lt.	Usurper	DSC
Mott H.A.	L. Sto.	Trooper	MID
Mott H.E.	C.P.O.	Thames	
Motteram T.G.	A.B.	Shakespeare	
Moulder E.T.	Ord. Sea.	P.33	
Mowbray F.T.	L. Sto.	Olympus	
Mudd T.E.	Sup. P.O.	Undaunted	
Mudge F.S.	Sto. 1	Odin	
Mullens J.H.	Ch. Era.	Regulus	
Munday E.	Sto. 2	Upholder	
Munns S.W.T.	A.B.	H.31	
Munro H.C.S.	A.B.	Virtue	
Munro W.	L. Sto.	Snapper	
Muntz Sir G.P.G.	Lt.	Regulus	
Murdoch A.	Sto. 1	Tetrarch	
Murgatroyd S.E.	P.O.	Thames	
Murphy J.	Sto. 1	Tuna	
Murphy K.C.	Tel.	Regent	
Murray A.J.	L. Tel.	Regent	
Murray G.N.	L. Tel.	Thunderbolt	
Murray N.B.	Era. 3	P.222	
Murray R.	Sto. 2	P.514	
Murray T.H.	Era. 3	Thistle	
Musgrave A.	Tel.	P.514	
Musgrove W.C.	Tel.	Talisman	
Nash J.R.	A.B.	Porpoise	
Neale A.F.M.	P.O.	Olympus	
Neale P.T.	L. Sig.	Perseus	
Neale R.H.	P.O.	Stonehenge	
Neel-Wall M.N.	Lt.	Tempest	
Neilson T.P.	Era. 4	Talisman	
Nelson L.C.	L. Sea.	Traveller	
Nesbitt W.F.	A.B.	P.311	
Nesling R.A.	L. Sig.	Snapper	
Nettleton J.	Ch. Era.	Sickle	
Neville R.W.P.	L. Sto.	Triumph	
Neville W.H.	A.B.	Triumph	
Newberry E.	L. Sea.	Traveller	
Newby G.	A.B.	Triumph	
Newcomb J.E.	A.B.	Thunderbolt	
Newell D.E.T.	Lt. RNR	Thames	
Newell F.	A.B.	Narwhal	
Newell R.J.H.	A.B.	Traveller	
Newland G.T.	Suppy. Asst.	Olympus	
Newland J.L.	L. Sto.	Thorn	
Newlands P. Mac.C.	Tel.	Upholder	
Newman F.C.	Sto. 1	Thunderbolt	
Newman R.T.	Era. 5	P.222	
Newman W.J.	Era. 1	Tetrarch	
Newton A.E.	Sto. 1	Undaunted	
Newton A.S.	A.B.	P.311	
Newton R.	L. Sto.	Thunderbolt	
Newton W.	Sig.	Utmost	
Nichol H.	Era. 4	Untamed	
Nicholay E.C.F.	Lt. Cmdr.	Perseus	
Nicholl D.E.	S. Lt. RNVR	P.615	
Nichols R.T.	A.B.	Swordfish	
Nicholson E.G.	A.B.	Grampus	
Nicholson G.B.	L. Sto.	Sterlet	
Nicholson G.S.	Lt. (E) RNR	Tigris	
Nicholson J.E.	L. Tel.	Traveller	
Nicholson L.F.	Sto. 1	Tigris	
Niel S.M.	A.B.	Unique	
Noble G.P.	Era. 4	Regent	
Noll G.M.	Lt.	Untamed	
Noone E.	Sto. 1	Grampus	
Norfolk R.G.	Lt. Cmdr.	Thorn	DSO
Norman J.H.	S. Lt. RNVR	Upholder	DSC
Norris J.	L. Sea.	Urge	
Norris P.W.G.	L. Sea.	Regulus	
Norris R.D.	C.P.O.	Unbeaten	DSM
Norris W.T.	Era. 3	Tetrarch	MID
North W.	L. Sea.	Orpheus	

Northcott L.H.J.	Sto. P.O.	Grampus	
Northover McK. T.	Y. of S.	Tetrarch	
Northwood A.	P.O. Tel.	Swordfish	
Norwood R.J.	Sto. 1	Thunderbolt	
Nott R.	C.P.O.	Triumph	
Nowell G.H.	Lt. Cmdr.	Phoenix	
Nunn A.	Era. 4	Parthian	
Nutall W.	Elec. Art. 4	Thorn	
Nutt W.	Sto. 1	Tigris	
Nuttall J.H.	Elec. Art. 3	Sterlet	
Oakes H.G.	P.O. Tel.	Talisman	
Oates L.C.	L. Sea.	Turbulent	
O'Brien B.E.	Lt. Cmdr. (E)	Thames	
O'Brien C.	A.B.	Traveller	
O'Brien C.	P.O. Ck. (s)	Triumph	
O'Brien W.A.	L. Tel.	H.31	
O'Carroll T.C.	A.B.	Syrtis	
O'Connor J.	A.B.	Tigris	
Odam S.G.	L. Stwd.	Traveller	
O'Dowd M.	L. Tel.	P.551	
Ogden C.	A.B.	Turbulent	
Ogilvy W.D.E.	Lt.	Unbeaten	DSC
O'Haire E.E.P.	Era. 3	Spearfish	
O'Hare D.A.	Lt.	Usk	
O'Hare J.	Era. 2	P.615	
Olding W.G.	Ch. Era.	Simoon	
Oldridge F.W.J.	Sto. 1	Perseus	
O'Leary M.T.	Elec. Art. 3	Simoon	
Oliffe J.	A.B.	Porpoise	
Oliver A.G.			
Oliver D.L.B.	L. Sto.	Unbeaten	MID
Oliver O.	Era. 3	Spearfish	
Oliver T.	Sto. 1	Porpoise	
llerenshaw D.	A.B.	P.615	
Olrog E.W.	Sto. 1	Odin	
'Mahoney M.	Sto. 1	Salmon	
merod M.	A.B.	Turbulent	
'Neill J.	A.B.	Urge	MID
'Neill J.P.	Sto. 1	Swordfish	
'Reilly J.	L. Tel.	Union	
'Riordan D.	L. Sto.	Perseus	
rme S.	Sto. 1	Triton	
rell J.	L. Sto.	Usk	
rrom W.S.	P.O.	Splendid	
rton M.S.	S. Lt.	P.48	
sborn H.G.A.	L. Sea.	Urge	DSM
sman F.	P.O.	Syrtis	
swald W.H.	Era. 4	Scotsman	
tignon C.V.	A.B.	Salmon	
uthwaite E.	Sto. 1	Tigris	
ver W.	Sto. 1	Olympus	
wen B.	A.B.	Traveller	
wen R.	Elec. Art. 1	Thames	
wen R.P.G.	Lt. RNR	P.39	
wens W.J.	L. Sto.	Thistle	
xborrow C.E.	Lt.	Unshaken	DSC
xley E.G.	P.O.	Perseus	
xley G.	Tel.	Vandal	
xley J.H.	Era. 4	P.615	
ce W.J.	P.O. Tel.	Stonehenge	
cker J.W.	A.B.	Regent	
cker W.M.H.	Era. 3	Seahorse	
ge L.H.	Ch. Era.	Utmost	
ge S.E.	Era. 4	Syrtis	

Paige J.C.	Lt. RNR	Sterlet	
Pain R.M.E.	Lt. Cmdr.	P.514	
Painter C.F.	Era. 3	Thames	
Pallister H.	L. Sto.	Orpheus	
Pallister H.	L. Sto.	Porpoise	
Palmer G.	C.P.O. Tel.	Salmon	
Palmer G.W.	Tel.	Parthian	
Palmer H.J.	Era. 1	Rainbow	
Palmer S.	A.B.	Snapper	
Palmer S.	Sto. P.O.	Traveller	
Palmer W.H.	S. Lt.	Oxley	
Pardoe C.A.	Lt. RNR	Parthian	
Parfitt W.F.	P.O.	P.222	
Paris F.J.S.	Sto. P.O.	Traveller	
Parish J.C.	L. Sto.	Narwhal	MID
Parker A.E.	L. Sto.	Grampus	
Parker C.	Era. 3	Phoenix	
Parker C.J.	Lt. RNVR	Thorn	
Parker J.K.	Era. 3	Thames	
Parker J.W.	L. Tel.	Rainbow	
Parker K.H.	A.B.	Parthian	
Parker W.T.	L. Tel.	Syrtis	
Parkinson J.L.	A.B.	Urge	
Parkinson P.R.	A.B.	Traveller	
Parramore W.A.	L. Sto.	Triton	
Parratt M.B.	A.B.	Thames	
Parris S.G.	Elec. Art. 4	Regent	
Parry O.	L. Sea.	Phoenix	
Parsons G.E.H.	L. Ck. (o)	Tempest	
Parsons V.J.	L. Sto.	Snapper	DSM
Parsons W.	Era. 4	Tetrarch	
Pashley P.W.	Era. 3	Grampus	
Passmore J.	P.O. Tel.	Porpoise	
Paterson E.	A.B.	Salmon	
Paterson J.A.	Sto. 1	Thorn	
Paterson J.G.W.	Ch. Era.	Tarpon	
Paton J.H.T.	A.B.	Pandora	
Patrick D.	Era. 4	Stratagem	
Patterson H.	Tel.	P.514	
Patterson J.B.	A.B.	Stonehenge	
Paul C.N.	L. Ck. (s)	Thorn	
Paulyn W.F.J.	L. Sto.	Rainbow	
Paxford F.J.	Sto. P.O.	Phoenix	
Paxton A.A.	C.P.O. Tel.	Grampus	
Paxton R.W.	Sto. 1	P.222	
Payne C.E.H.	C.P.O.	Traveller	DSM
Payne G.C.C.	Sup. P.O.	Phoenix	
Peacock C.C.	L. Sto.	Perseus	
Pearce A.J.	L. Sea.	P.48	
Pearce C.H.	L. Sea.	Turbulent	MID
Pearce L.W.	P.O. Tel.	Stratagem	
Pearson A.	Tel.	Union	
Pearson E.	Sto. 1	Olympus	
Pearson J.T.	Sto. 1	Sickle	
Pearson W.	Sto. P.O.	Tetrarch	
Pearson W.G.	L. Sto.	Olympus	
Peck G.A.	A.B.	Olympus	
Peebles W.C.	Y. of S.	Turbulent	MID
Peel S.N.	Era. 1	Spearfish	DSM
Pegler F.	Wrnt. Engr.	Phoenix	
Pelly C.R.	Lt.	Stratagem	DSC
Pendleton R.G.	Sto. 1	Untamed	
Penfold L.C.H.	Ch. Era.	Orpheus	
Penn A.E.	P.O. Tel.	Thistle	

Penny R.R.	L. Sea.	Snapper	
Penny W.F.A.	L. Sig.	Sturgeon	
Pepper W.E.	L. Sea.	Tetrarch	
Pepper W.R.	P.O. Tel.	P.615	
Perham D.	Sto. 1	Seahorse	
Perkin W.S.	P.O.	Thistle	
Perkins F.W.	L. Sto.	Upholder	
Perkins L.W.	L. Tel.	Tarpon	
Perry E.G.	A.B.	Orpheus	
Perry J.C.	Sto. 1	Regent	
Perry W.J.	A.B.	Regulus	
Peterkin A.J.	Lt.	Triumph	
Peterkin C.H.	Lt.	H.49	
Peters M.	Era. 4	Trooper	
Peterson A J.	L. Sig.	Thames	
Petoltenaere A.	Sto. 2	Narval (Fr.)	
Pettitt G.R.	Sto. 1	Triton	
Phelps R.H.	Sto. P.O.	Orpheus	
Phillimore W.A.	Lt.	P.514	
Phillips A.D.	Tel.	Phoenix	
Phillips F.J.	Sto. 1	Rainbow	
Phillips F.J.J.	A.B.	Stratagem	
Phillips J.H.R.	P.O.	Vandal	
Phillips P.R.	Lt. (E)	Tetrarch	
Phillips T.	Ch. Era.	Triumph	
Phillips V.G.	Sto. 1	Umpire	
Phipps J.C.	L. Sto.	Seahorse	
Pickard H.	P.O.	Stratagem	
Pickard J.B.	Era. 1	Sterlet	
Pickering W.	A.B.	Oxley	
Pickers A.E.	A.B.	Regent	
Picknell W.G.	L. Sea.	Syrtis	
Pickthall T.	Sto. 1	Orpheus	
Pickvance S.F.O.	L. Sea.	Traveller	
Pidgeon S.A.	Lt.	P.38	
Pike G.E.F.	L. Sea.	Olympus	
Pike R.F.	Ord. Sea.	Usurper	
Pilkington F.	L. Sea.	Rainbow	
Pilton F.J.	A.B.	Splendid	MID
Pinkney H.	Sto. 1	Traveller	
Piper A.E.	L. Tel.	Unbeaten	
Piper R.W.J.	L. Sto.	Olympus	
Pirie D.A.	Lt.	Spearfish	DSO
Plant B.	Sto. 1	Usk	
Plant D.F.	Era. 4	Perseus	
Plant S.	Era. 3	Olympus	
Playfair P.	L. Tel.	Untamed	
Plested E.	Sto. 1	Swordfish	
Plumb C.	Sto. P.O.	Snapper	
Pook I. L. R.	L. Sea.	Triton	
Poole J.M.S.	Lt.	Urge	DSC*
Pope F.E.	P.O.	Sickle	
Pope J.E.	Sto. 1	Thorn	
Popham W.H.	L. Sea	Sterlet	
Porteous K.	Sto. 1	P.38	
Porteous T.H.	Sto. P.O.	Triad	
Porter R.E.	A.B.	Thorn	
Porter W.H.	P.O. Tel.	Usk	
Portman J.M.B.	Lt.	Vandal	
Potter D.W.	Era. 4	Parthian	
Potter P.A.G.	Sto. P.O.	Triumph	
Powell J.H.	L. Sea.	Phoenix	
Powell R.H.	P.O. Tel.	Syrtis	
Powell R.W.W.	A.B.	P.514	
Powell T.J.	Sto. 1	Stonehenge	
Powell W.J.	A.B.	Orpheus	
Power L.	Sto. 1	Salmon	
Poxon R.W.	A.B.	Olympus	
Pratt E.J.C.	Wrnt. Engr.	Regent	
Preddy L.J.	L. Sto.	Swordfish	
Preddy T.N.	Sto. P.O.	Perseus	
Preece D.J.	A.B.	Thunderbolt	
Prentice C.E.	S. Lt. RNVR	Stratagem	
Preston B.H.	L. Sto.	Stratagem	
Pretty R.	A.B.	Regulus	
Price A.K.	Sup. P.O.	Parthian	
Price H.R.	L. Tel.	P.615	
Price I.T.	Sto. 1	Olympus	
Price R.	Sto. 1	Traveller	
Price T.	Ch. Era.	Thorn	DSM
Pridham R.W.B.	Sto. 1	P.311	
Prince F.W.	Sto. 1	Thunderbolt	
Pringle N.	Sto. P.O.	Regulus	
Print G.E.	L. Sea.	P.32	
Prior T.W.F.	Sto. 1	Narwhal	
Pritchard H.	A.B.	Tempest	
Proudfoot A.P.	L. Sea.	Porpoise	BEM
Prowse G.V.	Lt.	Snapper	
Pughe A.	P.O. Tel.	Seahorse	
Puttick E.A.T.	Ch. Era.	Olympus	
Pym W.J.	A.B.	Tigris	
Quarrell W.H.	P.O.	Tigris	
Quayle W.H.	Sto. 1	Usurper	
Quested H.A.	L. Sea.	Tetrarch	
Quick G.	Sto. 1	Triton	
Quin C.G.	L. Sea.	Narwhal	MID
Quinn M.	Sto. 1	P.311	
Radwell P.F.J.	Lt.	Stonehenge	
Rae T.	A.B.	Thistle	
Raggett A.F.	Ch. Sto.	Tarpon	
Ralphson S.	Tel.	Undaunted	
Ramsey R.S.	Sto. 1	Traveller	
Randall P.R.	A.B.	Usk	
Randell V.C.	C.P.O.	Phoenix	
Ranken T.A.	L. Tel.	Porpoise	
Ransome J.S.D.	Lt. RNR	Urge	DSC
Ranson W.A.	Sto. 1	Triumph	
Ratcliffe M.E.P.	Lt.	Swordfish	
Rawe J.A.	C.P.O.	Simoon	
Rawlings A.E.	P.O.	Regent	
Rawlings A.T.	L. Sto.	Spearfish	
Rawlings H.C.E.	L. Sea.	Salmon	
Rayner B.W.F.	P.O.	Usurper	DSM
Rayner F.S.	Wrnt. Engr.	Stratagem	
Rayner P.M.	Era. 4	Olympus	
Raynor L.J.	L. Sea.	Tigris	
Read A.G.	L. Sig.	Untamed	
Reading J.F.	A.B.	Thistle	
Rear F.	Sto. 1	Tempest	
Redding R.F.J.	A.B.	Grampus	
Redman J.	Sto. 1	Trusty	
Redman J.W.	L. Sea.	P.311	
Reed C.I.	S. Lt.	Unique	
Reed E.R.	A.B.	Traveller	
Rees J.E.	A.B.	Stonehenge	
Rees T.J.	Sto. 1	Perseus	
Reeson F.	L. Sea.	Orpheus	
Reeson R.C.	L. Sto.	Thorn	

Reeve B.P.	Sto. 1	Olympus	
Reeves J.G.	P.O.	Undaunted	
Reeves R.H.	A.B.	Turbulent	DSM MID
Regan R.J.	P.O. Tel.	Olympus	
Regent H.F.	Era. 4	Triumph	
Reid G.W.A.	L. Sto.	Traveller	
Reilly J.	A.B.	Urchin	
Relf J.H.	Sto. 1	Phoenix	
Render J.	Tel.	Perseus	
Render O.	A.B.	Usurper	
Rennie C.M.	Ord. Sea.	Tigris	
Rescorla J.A.	A.B. RNVR	Olympus	
Revington F.	Ord. Sea.	Vandal	
Reynolds W.	L. Tel.	H.50	
Rhodes B.G.	L. Sea.	Regent	
Ribbands R.	Ord. Sea.	P.311	
Ribbans S.E.	P.O. Tel.	Trooper	
Rice S.	A.B.	Thunderbolt	
Richards B.	A.B.	Tetrarch	
Richards J.C.	A.B.	H.31	
Richards T.G.	Sto. 1	Tetrarch	
Richards W.G.	L. Sig.	Thistle	
Richardson A.	A.B.	Syrtis	
Richardson C.G.	L. Sea.	Perseus	
Richardson F.	Sto. 1	Grampus	
Richardson J.	A.B.	Stratagem	
Richardson J.B.G.	L. Sea.	Regulus	
Richardson T.S.	A.B.	Porpoise	
Richardson W.	A.B.	Usk	
Richardson W.	L. Tel.	Turbulent	
Richlieu T.W.	Tel.	Narwhal	
Richman S.L.	C.P.O.	Tigris	MID
Rickberry I.	Sto. 1	Triad	
Ricks P.A.	Tel.	P.222	
Rickwood B.G.S.	L. Sea.	P.311	
Ridley R.R.	A.B.	Turbulent	MID
Riley L.J.	L. Sea.	Unique	
Rimmington A.N.V.	S. Lt. RNVR	Sealion	DSM
Ringham F.	C.P.O.	Thunderbolt	
Ripley J.	Sto. 1	Olympus	
Ritchens S.H.	A.B.	Stratagem	
Robbins R.H.H.	L. Sto.	Triad	
Roberts D.D.G.	Lt.	Porpoise	MID
Roberts F.	Tel.	Tigris	
Roberts G.	A.B.	Grampus	
Roberts H.M.	Era. 2	Orpheus	
Roberts J.T.	Ord. Sea.	P.32	
Roberts J.W.	Sto. 1	Usurper	
Roberts N.	L. Sig.	Undaunted	
Roberts R.	A.B.	Umpire	
Robertson A.M.	L. Sto.	Regulus	
Robertson A.S.	Lt.	Perseus	
Robertson F.S.	L. Sto.	Orpheus	
Robertson F.S.	Seaman RNR	Perseus	
Robertson J.M.	Era. 3	Stonehenge	
Robertson R.W.C.	Wrnt. Engr.	Oxley	
Robertson W.	A.B.	Olympus	
Robinson A.	Sto. 1	Triumph	
Robinson A.H.	L. Tel.	P.38	
Robinson B.H.G.	Ch. Era.	Rainbow	
Robinson F.C.O.	L. Sea.	Usk	
Robinson H.	L. Sea.	Phoenix	
Robinson H.E.	Era. 4	Traveller	
Robinson N.	P.O.	Narwhal	
Robinson R.N.	L. Sto.	Trooper	DSM
Robinson W.	A.B.	Talisman	
Robinson W.T.	P.O.	Grampus	
Robson R.	A.B.	Odin	
Robson T.R.	Era. 4	Talisman	
Rodham J.T.	P.O.	Satyr	
Rodwell R.H.	A.B.	Usurper	
Rogers B.V.	Sto. 1	P.222	
Rogers P.	A.B.	Porpoise	
Rogers R.	P.O.	Porpoise	MID
Rogers R.W.G.	L. Tel.	Urge	
Rogers R.W.M.	L. Sea.	Undaunted	
Rolfe W.H.	A.B.	Stonehenge	
Rollet J.M.	A.B.	Narval (Fr.)	
Rollins S.E.	Era. 4	H.31	
Rolph D.	C.P.O.	Sickle	
Ronald G.H.	A.B.	P.38	
Roose G.W.	L. Sea.	Sickle	
Rosendale E.D.	Sto. 1	Triumph	
Rosenwarne W.A.	A.B.	Snapper	
Ross A.	Sto. P.O.	Narwhal	
Ross M.	A.B.	Traveller	
Ross P.G.	L. Sto.	Odin	
Round O.C.	Lt.	Regulus	
Rouse L.J.A.	A.B.	Tigris	
Rousell W.R.	Sto. 1	Thistle	
Rowe C.A.	Lt. Cmdr.	Grampus	
Rowe J.	L. Sto.	Upholder	
Rowland J.	A.B.	Tetrarch	
Rowlands G.	A.B.	Porpoise	
Rowlett F.	A.B.	Tigris	
Rowley J.K.	A.B.	Urge	DSM
Royle R.	Sto. P.O.	Spearfish	
Ruck K.F.	Lt.	Upholder	DSC
Rudge C.H.	A.B.	P.311	
Rumble J.	P.O.	Parthian	
Rundle N.J.	L. Sea.	Tigris	
Rush W.G.A.	A.B.	Traveller	
Russell D.	Era. 4	Stonehenge	
Russell E.R.W.	Era. 3	Regent	
Ruston B.T.	L. Sea.	Trooper	
Rutter R.F.	Elec. Art. 4	Urge	
Ryan T.R.	Sto. 1	Thames	
Ryder J.S.	S. Lt. RNVR	Trooper	
Sabbe St. L.A.R.	Lt.	Tigris	
Sainsbury G.W.	Sto. 1	Trooper	
Salles R.	A.B.	Narval (Fr.)	
Salmon A.W.	A.B.	Simoon	
Salt B.F.	L. Sea.	Orpheus	
Salt G.S.	Lt. Cmdr.	Triad	
Salter AJ	L. Sto.	P.222	
Salter C.H.	A.B.	P.38	
Sampson R.G.	Lt.	Tigris	DSC
Sanders J.A.	P.O. Tel.	Tempest	
Sanders W.	A.B.	Oxley	
Sant A.W.J.	L. Sto.	Porpoise	
Sarfas A.S.	Commd. Engr.	Sterlet	
Sargant W.C.R.	L. Sto.	Sterlet	
Sargeant K.I.	L. Tel.	Stonehenge	
Sargent J.	Lt. RNVR	P.311	
Saunders A.	A.B.	Simoon	
Saunders F.	A.B.	Thunderbolt	
Saunders H.E.	L. Sto.	P.222	

Saunders L.	L. Sea.	Upholder	
Saunders L.R.	Sto. P.O.	Thistle	
Saunderson E.P.	P.O.	Triton	DSM
Savage S.A.	L. Sto.	Regent	
Savill K.A.P.	A.B.	Splendid	
Sawyer G.A.	L. Sig.	Regent	
Saxby T.R.	A.B.	Triton	
Scanlan J.	L. Sto.	P.222	
Scard R.J.	Sto. 1	P.32	
Scarlett J.	L. Sto.	Odin	
Scarlett L. A.	Tel.	P.48	
Schofield B.P.	A.B.	Simoon	
Scholes J.	Era. 4	Traveller	
Schroder J.C.	Ch. Era.	P.38	
Schuil A.E.	Lt. RNVR	P.615	
Scott C.	A.B.	Grampus	
Scott T.N.	C.P.O.	Orpheus	
Scott W.	L. Sto.	P.512	
Scott W.	Sto. P.O.	Tetrarch	
Scouse E.O.	A.B.	P.38	
Seaborne W.J.	Sto. 1	Simoon	
Seal R.A.	L. Sto.	Utmost	
Searle F.W.	A.B.	Usurper	
Seddon D.	Sto. 1	Trooper	
Seeley H.	L. Stwd.	Pandora	
Self E.E.	Sto. 1	Upholder	
Selway H.T.	Wrnt. Engr.	Swordfish	
Seymour R.N.G.	L. Sto.	Sickle	
Shanahan J.	A.B.	Utmost	
Shanks T.S.	S. Lt. RNVR	Simoon	
Sharp N.	A.B.	Simoon	
Sharp W.E.	Sto. P.O.	Turbulent	DSM
Sharples G.F.	A.B.	Tetrarch	
Shaw G.C.F.	A.B.	P.615	
Shaw W.	Sto. 1	Regulus	
Shears F.	Sto. 1	Triton	
Sheldon C.A.	Sto. P.O.	Triumph	BEM MID
Shelley G.A.	Asst. Stwd.	Triad	
Shelton C.	Sto. 1	Unity	
Shepherd H.	A.B.	Vandal	
Shepherd H.W.J.	Era. 1	Vandal	
Shepherd J.V.	L. Sto.	Simoon	
Shepherdson G.R.	A.B.	Thames	
Sherrick J.	A.B.	Sterlet	
Sherriff J.	Tel.	Porpoise	
Sherry R.W.	Commd. Engr.	Tarpon	
Shields T.H.	Ord. Sea.	Syrtis	
Shimmin J.	L. Sea.	Triton	
Shinn V.T.	Elec. Art. 3	Tetrarch	
Shipley E.	L. Stwd.	Tempest	
Shipley J.H.N.	A.B.	Swordfish	
Shipley P.	Sto. 1	P.38	
Shoebridge S.H.	L. Tel.	Trooper	
Short H.C.	L. Sto.	P.311	
Shoulder G.E.	A.B.	Regent	
Siddell J.S.	L. Sto.	Thistle	
Sidebotham H.	Sto. 1	Odin	
Silver R.H.S.	Lt.	P.311	
Sim J.	A.B.	P.45	
Simcox W.E.	L. Sea.	Triad	
Simmonds R.	L. Sig.	Upholder	
Simmons J.F.	Sto. 1	Tetrarch	
Simmons R.D.C.G.	Lt.	Union	

Simnett S.	L. Sto.	Narwhal	
Simons T.W.	P.O.	Utmost	DSM* MID
Simpkins G.A.	P.O.	Porpoise	
Simpson F.D.	Sto. 1	H.49	
Simpson F.E.	Sto. 1	Narwhal	
Simpson H.	L. Sea.	Thistle	
Simpson M.	Era. 4	Turbulent	MID
Simpson R.R.	Lt.	Odin	
Simpson W.R.	A.B.	Thunderbolt	
Sinclair A.D.	Lt.	Sickle	
Sinclair J.	A.B.	P.615	
Sinden A.	P.O. Tel.	Odin	
Skelt K.D.	Lt.	Salmon	
Skeoch J. McK.	A.B.	Porpoise	
Skilling A.A.V.	P.O.	Seahorse	
Skinner H.	L. Ck. (s)	Trooper	
Skinner R.W.	A.B.	Regent	
Skinner W.	Sto. P.O.	Triad	
Skippon G.L.	L. Ck. (s)	P.311	
Slade P.D.	Elec. Art. 4	Pandora	
Slater W.	L. Sto.	P.615	
Sleep R.B.	P.O.	Trooper	DSM
Smallwood T.J.	L. Sea.	Usurper	
Smedley F.	A.B.	Usurper	
Smethurst F.	A.B.	Trooper	
Smith A.	A.B.	H.31	
Smith A.C.	L. Sea.	P.615	DSM
Smith A.C.S.	Era. 3	Seahorse	
Smith A.G.	P.O.	Spearfish	
Smith A.G.	Sto. 1	Porpoise	
Smith A.H.	Tel.	P.33	
Smith C.C.	A.B.	Seal	
Smith C.G.	A.B.	Unbeaten	
Smith E.	Sto. 1	Spearfish	
Smith E.D.	L. Sea.	Regulus	
Smith E.S.	A.B.	Odin	
Smith E.W.	Tel.	Spearfish	
Smith F.	P.O. Ck.	Porpoise	
Smith F.W.	A.B.	Tetrarch	
Smith G.	Era. 4	Tigris	
Smith G.A.	A.B.	Traveller	
Smith G.E.R.	A.B.	Upholder	
Smith G.W.J.	L. Sea.	Pandora	
Smith J.	A.B.	Upholder	
Smith J.	Era. 4	Porpoise	
Smith J.	L. Sea.	Tarpon	
Smith J.	Sto. 1	Narwhal	
Smith J.	Tel.	Olympus	
Smith J. F.	P.O. Tel.	Regulus	
Smith J.M.	Era. 3	Spearfish	MID
Smith J.R.	L. Sto.	Triad	
Smith L.G.	P.O. Tel.	Untamed	
Smith L.J.	A.B.	Porpoise	
Smith L.S.	Era. 4	Splendid	
Smith M.J.R.	Lt.	Triton	MID
Smith N.A.	Sto. 1	Grampus	
Smith P.R.	Sto. 2	Porpoise	
Smith R.	A.B.	Stonehenge	
Smith R.	Shpt. 3	Regulus	
Smith S.T.	Sto. P.O.	P.33	
Smith T.H.	L. Sea.	Rainbow	
Smith W.	Sto. 1	Rainbow	
Smith W.J.	Sto. 1	Simoon	

Smithard R.M.	S. Lt.	P.32	
Smithson J.	A.B.	Parthian	
Smithson J.A.	L. Sto.	Thorn	
Smyth T.	P.O.	Triton	
Smythe H.A.	L. Tel.	Phoenix	
Snell N.E.	Era. 3	Stratagem	
Snell S.R.	Sto. 1	Tarpon	
Soanes J.W.	A.B.	Tigris	
Soar P.A.	Sto. 1	H.49	
Songhurst T.J.	Sto. 1	Simoon	
Souris E.G.	Sto. 1	Swordfish	
South A.	Sto. 1	P.615	
Southwell A.W.	P.O. Ck. (s)	Thames	
Sowden W.	Ord. Sea.	Usk	
Sparrow W.J.	Ch. Era.	P.33	
Speed F.A.	A.B.	Parthian	NZ
Spencer A.	Sto. 1	Untamed	
Spencer D.	P.O.	H.31	
Spencer E.R.	L. Sto.	Porpoise	
Spencer K.H.	A.B.	Tetrarch	NZ
Spender E.H.	L. Sto.	Stonehenge	
Spettigue J.H.	Sig.	O.13 (Dutch)	
Spice R.W.	Era. 4	Thunderbolt	
Spite K.F.	Seaman RNR	Triton	
Spittle E.T.	Era. 2	Union	DSM
Spittles E.V.	Sto. 1	Salmon	
Spouse A.	L. Sto.	Phoenix	
Spowart A.	Ch. Sto.	Tempest	
Spratt F.E.	Lt.	Syrtis	
Spring R.S.E.	Lt. RNVR	P.48	
Sproat D.J.	Sto. 1	Swordfish	
Spurden E.G.V.	L. Sea.	Tarpon	
Spurgeon H.V.	Era. 2	Swordfish	
Squire A.J.	Ch. Sto.	P.311	
St. Clair-Ford D.	Lt. Cmdr.	Traveller	
Stacey H.A.	Lt.	Swordfish	
Staff J.	Tel.	Olympus	
Stafford F.T.	A.B.	Triton	
Staines A.F.	L. Sea.	P.222	
Stamper J. McG.	L. Sto.	H.31	
Stanger M.	Sto. 1	Urge	
Stanley C.	Sto. 1	Thunderbolt	
Stanley P.J.	L. Sto.	Unbeaten	DSM
Stanley S.J.	Sto. 2	Perseus	
Stanley V.A.	Ord. Sea.	P.222	
Stannard J.L.	L. Sea.	Rainbow	
Stanton S.C.	A.B.	Seahorse	
Stanton W.H.	Sto. 2	Vandal	
Stanway F.W.	A.B.	Stratagem	
Stapleton R.R.	Ord. Sea.	Vandal	
Stapley E.W.	Era. 4	Swordfish	
Stark T.A.	Era. 3	Sickle	
Starkey J.E.	Ord. Tel.	Parthian	
Starrett E.T.	Ch. Era.	P.615	
Staveley J.R.	A.B.	Phoenix	
Stavert D.R.	Lt.	Tetrarch	
Stead J.	A.B.	Turbulent	MID
Stearn G.R.	A.B.	Narwhal	
Steel S.	A.B.	Syrtis	
Steele J.M.	Era. 4	P.514	
Stephens H.	Era. 4	Triumph	
Stevens F.A.	Ch. Era.	Tempest	
Stevens N.C.	A.B.	Sickle	
Stevens R.	A.B.	H.49	
Stevenson L.	A.B.	Oxley	
Steventon A.	L. Sto.	Seahorse	
Stewart A.	P.O.	Snapper	
Stewart F.A.J.	Sto. 1	Parthian	
Stewart J.R.	L. Sea.	Sickle	
Stewart W.R.	L. Sea.	P.32	
Stillwell C.J.	L. Ck. (s)	Trooper	
Stinchcombe C.A.	L. Sea.	Grampus	
Stinton F.A.	L. Sto.	Rainbow	
Stobbie J.	Tel.	Trooper	
Stockham W.H.	Ch. Sto.	Triumph	BEM DSM*
Stockwell J. E.F.	L. Sto.	Unbeaten	DSM
Stokes J.	A.B.	Usk	
Stokes J.	Sto. 1	Thames	
Stone C.P.	Sto. 1	Tetrarch	
Stone C.W.	Sto. 1	Narwhal	
Stone F.P. de M.	A.B.	Turbulent	
Stone H.	Tel.	Triumph	
Storey D.	Sto. 1	Grampus	
Storey F.A.	A.B.	Syrtis	
Storr J.W.	P.O. Tel.	P.222	
Stott E.	Era. 4	Trooper	
Stovell E.J.	A.B.	Olympus	
Stradling J.H.	L. Ck.	Odin	
Stranaghan H.	L. Sto.	Turbulent	
Straw C.	Sto. 1	Snapper	
Strawbridge R.J.	Tel.	Orpheus	
Street F.C.A.	Sto. 2	Talisman	
Stretton-Smith G.	Lt. RNVR	P.311	
Stribbling W.A.	Tel.	Thames	
Stride C.J.F.	A.B.	Triton	
Stroud R.P.	L. Tel.	Salmon	
Stuart G.C.E.	Lt.	Taku	
Stubbington W.J.	L. Sto.	Narwhal	
Stubbs G.J.	Ch. Era.	Syrtis	DSM
Sturgess M.V.	Sto. 1	Sickle	
Sturman T.G.	L. Sto.	Unbeaten	
Styles W.J.	Ord. Sea.	P.32	
Sullivan P.J.	L. Sto.	Talisman	
Sumby G.W.	P.O.	P.615	
Summers E.R.S.	Elec. Art. 3	Seahorse	
Summers J.	Sto. 1	Phoenix	
Summers O.J.	Era. 3	Salmon	
Summers S.L.	Ch. Era.	Union	
Summersbee J.F.	P.O.	Thistle	
Sumner F.	A.B.	Umpire	
Sumner H.G.	S. Lt. RNVR	Trooper	
Sumpton R.R.	Seaman RNR	Undaunted	
Surq M.	Sig.	Narval (Fr.)	
Sutch H.V.A.	Sto. 1	Usk	
Sutherland W.F.	A.B.	P.311	
Sutton R.J.	Lt. RNVR	Regent	
Sutton T.H.	Sto. P.O.	Usurper	
Swainston J.G.	C.P.O.	Upholder	DSM*
Swallow A.G.	L. Sto.	Salmon	
Swann E.E.	A.B.	P.615	
Sweeney J.	Sto. 1	Turbulent	
Sweetman W.	Sto. P.O.	Odin	
Swift G.H.J.	Tel.	Grampus	
Sykes J.C.	Era. 3	Parthian	
Sylvester E.	L. Sea.	Regulus	
Symonds J.D.	S. Lt.	Orpheus	
Symons L.H.	L. Sea.	Perseus	

Taaffe G.	Sto. 1	Usurper	
Tait J.	Lt. RNR	Perseus	
Talbot E.B.	Lt.	Snapper	
Talbot F.R.C.	Lt.	Thames	
Talbot L.E.	Era. 4	Odin	
Talbott F.G.	Era. 2	Olympus	
Tall C.	Era. 2	P.514	
Tallis R.G.	L. Sto.	Parthian	
Tame D.W.L.	Sto. 1	Trooper	
Tamplin D.W.E.	A.B.	Grampus	
Tancock S.J.	A.B.	P.222	
Tanner F.M.	Sto. P.O.	Tigris	
Targett A.L.J.	P.O.	Regulus	
Tarrant D.A.	Lt. RNR	Union	
Tatham B.P.	Sto. P.O.	Regent	
Tatlock J.	A.B.	Tarpon	
Taverner B.W.	S. Lt. RNVR	Utmost	
Tavolier L.E.	A.B.	Tetrarch	
Taylor A.	Sto. 1	Thames	
Taylor A.E.	P.O. Ck. (s)	P.615	DSM
Taylor A.J.D.	S. Lt.	P.222	
Taylor C.	A.B.	Usurper	
Taylor E.O.M.	Lt. RNVR	Porpoise	
Taylor G.	A.B.	Shakespeare	
Taylor J.	Era. 4	Simoon	
Taylor J.	Lt. RNR	P.514	
Taylor J.E.	A.B.	Triumph	
Taylor J.E.	L. Sto.	Regent	
Taylor L.F.	Wrnt. Engr.	P.222	
Taylor N.	Tel.	Thames	
Taylor R.	Sto. 1	Tetrarch	
Taylor R.E.	Sto. 1	Trooper	
Taylor V.	A.B.	Usurper	
Taylor V.F.	L. Sto.	Rainbow	
Taylor W.	Sto. 1	Traveller	
Templeton G.E.	Sto. 1	Tarpon	
Temporal A.	Tel.	Triton	
Terry F.W.	A.B.	Union	
Thain W.	Lt. RNR	Seahorse	
Theobald R.J.	P.O.	Triumph	DSM
Thewlis N.	A.B.	Unique	
Thomas C.J.	P.O.	Usk	
Thomas H.P.	L. Sig.	Stratagem	
Thomas J.	Lt.	Porpoise	
Thomas J.F.	L. Tel.	Tigris	
Thomas R.	L. Sea.	Porpoise	
Thomas R.A.S.H.	L. Tel.	Oxley	
Thomas W.N.C.	Sto. 1	Tarpon	
Thomas W.S.	Sto. 1	Triad	
Thompson E.H.	Tel.	Snapper	
Thompson F.	A.B.	Unbeaten	
Thompson F.R.	L. Sto.	Olympus	
Thompson J.H.	C.P.O.	Thistle	
Thompson L.	L. Tel.	Trooper	
Thompson L.W.	A.B.	Stratagem	
Thompson R.W.	Era. 4	Regent	
Thompson S.W.	Sto. 1	Phoenix	
Thompson T.E.	Sto. 1	Grampus	
Thompson W.R.	L. Sto.	Triad	
Thomsett H.G.	L. Sig.	Sterlet	
Thorn C.R.	A.B.	Unshaken	
Thorne W.F.	P.O.	Triton	
Thornhill A.A.	Sto. 1	Talisman	
Thornton R.	Sto. 1	Rainbow	

Thorpe A.G.	Sto. 1	Stratagem	
Thorpe R.	Wtr.	Olympus	
Tierney G.W.	L. Ck. (s)	Regent	
Tiffin L.	Era. 4	Unbeaten	
Tiley F.J.	L. Sea.	Oxley	
Timms F.J.	A.B.	Thames	
Tindall E.J.	P.O. Tel.	Thames	
Tippett W.	P.O.	Untamed	
Tivey J.	Sto. 1	Stonehenge	
Todd J.	Ch. Era.	Thistle	
Tolley G.M.	L. Sig.	Talisman	
Tolson S.	Y. of S.	Traveller	
Tombs G.W.	A.B.	Stonehenge	
Tomkinson E.P.	Lt. Cmdr.	Urge	DSO*
Toms C.H.	Ch. Era.	Urge	DSM
Tonks L.	L. Tel.	Swordfish	
Toogood J.W.	Sto. 1	Parthian	
Tooke D.P.	L. Sto.	Tigris	
Toombs R.	Era. 3	Sterlet	
Topping F.	L. Sto.	Upholder	
Torr H.	Y. of S.	Thorn	MID
Tott F.R.	P.O.	Orpheus	
Tovey G.C.	A.B.	P.615	
Town R.T.	L. Sto.	Umpire	
Trayhern L.F.	A.B.	Stonehenge	DSM
Traylor W.J.	Ord. Sea.	Thunderbolt	
Traynor W.M.	P.O. Tel.	Tapir	
Trebilcock R.C.	L. Sea.	Thames	
Trench J.	L. Sto.	Triton	
Trevethan B.	A.B.	P.311	
Trice W.A.	Ch. Era.	Regent	
Trier C.E.	S. Lt. RNVR	Porpoise	
Tripp F.W.	A.B.	Trooper	
Trott P.M.J.	Sto. 1	Tarpon	
Truckle M.T.	P.O.	H.31	
Trueman F.	A.B.	Olympus	
Tuck A.R.	C.P.O.	Unique	
Tucker O.M.	L. Tel.	Tigris	
Tugwell A.E.	P.O.	Sickle	
Tulip J.	L. Sto.	Odin	
Tulip T.E.	L. Sto.	Regulus	
Tunnell J.W.	Sto. 1	Turbulent	
Turnbull F.	A.B.	P.38	
Turnbull R.F.H.	L. Tel.	Unique	
Turner A.D.V.	L. Tel.	Regent	
Turner H.B.	Lt. Cmdr.	Porpoise	DSC
Turner J.J.	Sto. 1	Triumph	
Turner W.R.	P.O.	Upholder	DSM
Tuson G.W.	L. Tel.	Spearfish	
Tweed G.W.	Lt.	Rainbow	
Tweedy D.	A.B.	Unbeaten	
Tweedy T.C.	S. Lt.	Unbeaten	
Twiddy S.G.	L. Sea.	Usk	
Twine W.	Sto. 1	Regulus	
Twist H.E.	Tel.	Urge	
Twynam H.R.W.	Lt.	Narwhal	
Tyler W.J.	A.B.	Porpoise	
Underwood A.W.	Tel.	Oxley	
Underwood J.E.	A.B.	Triumph	
Undy J.	Era. 5	Snapper	
Upex F.A.E.	L. Sig.	Usurper	
Upton W.W.G.	A.B.	Thorn	
Usher R.R.H.	Lt.	Sentinel	
Vail A.H.	Sig.	P.615	

Varley E.	Era. 3	Urge	MID
Vass J.	L. Sea.	Thistle	
Vaughan F.J.	Era. 4	Porpoise	
Vaughan S.F.	Era. 5	Tantalus	
Venn L.J.	Tel.	Unique	
Venning L.C.	Sto. 1	Orpheus	
Verner-Jeffreys R.D.	Lt. (E)	Traveller	
Vernon A.	C.P.O.	Pandora	
Verschoyle-Campbell D.S.McN.	Lt.	Stonehenge	
Vincer G.W.	Sto. 1	Narwhal	
Vines R.S.	L. Sto.	Tigris	
Vokins C.H.	L. Sto.	P.311	
Von Bergen M.A.	Lt.	Parthian	
Voss P.R.J.	L. Tel.	Odin	
Waddell C. McT.	L. Sto.	Tempest	
Waddell R.	A.B.	Orpheus	
Waddington F.J.	A.B.	P.32	
Wainwright R.J.	Sto. P.O.	Tempest	
Waite F.	Sto. P.O.	Thames	
Walden R.B.	Tel.	Salmon	
Walford D.E.	P.O. Tel.	P.32	DSM
Walford L.	Lt. RNR	Pandora	
Walker C.R.	A.B.	Odin	
Walker H.F.	P.O.	Turbulent	
Walker H.W.	Sto. 1	Spearfish	
Walker J.T.R.	S. Lt. RNVR	Parthian	
Walker M.	Era. 2	Regulus	
Walker M.W.	L. Tel.	Salmon	
Walker P.G.	L. Sea.	Spearfish	
Walker R.B.	Sto. 1	Untamed	
Walker R.J.	L. Sto.	Tarpon	
Walker V.P.	S. Lt. RNVR	Sickle	
Wallace J.	L. Sto.	P.38	
Wallace J.	Sto. 1	P.615	
Wallen F.	Sto. 1	P.32	
Wallis A.E.	Ch. Era.	Grampus	
Wallis F.C.	Era. 4	Turbulent	
Wallis M.S.	Era. 2	Parthian	
Walmsley C.H.	Lt. RNR	Tetrarch	
Walmsley J.	L. Stwd.	Triumph	
Walsh J.J.	Sto. 1	Shark	
Walsh R.W.	Commd. Engr.	Tarpon	
Walters H.P.	C.P.O.	Thunderbolt	DSM
Walton L.	A.B.	Turbulent	
Walton W.S.H.	A.B.	Olympus	
Wanklyn M.D.	Lt. Cmdr.	Upholder	VC DSO**
Ward F.	Elec. Art. 1	Swordfish	MID
Ward F.A.C.G.	A.B.	Trooper	
Ward F.C.	Tel.	P.514	
Ward R.G.	Sto. P.O.	Saracen	DSM
Wardale I.G.	A.B.	Simoon	
Warden J.H.	L. Sto.	Thistle	
Wardle G.	Lt.	Sterlet	
Wardrop H.V.	C.P.O. Tel.	Perseus	
Warner A.	Ord. Sea.	P.33	
Warner H.F.	L. Sig.	Surcouf (Fr.)	
Warren G.E.	Elec. Art. 2	Phoenix	
Waterall G.D.	Midn.	Triumph	
Waterhouse G.A.			
Waterlow O.S.V.	Lt.	Talisman	DSC
Waters C.L.	Sto. 1	Oxley	
Waters C.P.	A.B.	Tempest	

Waters W.G.T.	A.B.	Triton	
Watkin J.H.	Elec. Art. 2	Grampus	
Watkins G.C.I.StB.	S. Lt.	Triton	
Watkins W.	L. Sto.	P.615	
Watson D.C.	Ch. Era.	Triton	
Watson E.	Sto. 1	Seahorse	
Watson J.	Sto. 1	Snapper	
Watson J.	Sto. 1	Stratagem	
Watson W.B.	A.B.	Oxley	
Watts E.H.	L. Sto.	Orpheus	
Watts H.R.J.	P.O.	Urge	DSM MID
Watts S.W.J.	Tel.	Pandora	
Waugh A.	A.B.	Tempest	
Way W.S.	Tel.	Odin	
Waye R.F.D.	L. Tel.	Triumph	DSM
Weatherall H.D.A.	S. Lt.	Tarpon	
Weatherhead R.G.	L. Ck. (s)	Stratagem	MID
Weatherley J.W.	P.O. Stwd.	Turbulent	
Weaver J.T.	Sig.	P.38	
Webb F.A.J.	A.B.	Thorn	
Webb F.J.	A.B.	Parthian	
Webb H.E.	A.B.	Oxley	
Webb J.H.T.	L. Sto.	Porpoise	
Webb P.J.	A.B.	Stratagem	
Webb R.P.	Lt.	Thunderbolt	
Webber G.M.	Tel.	Porpoise	
Webber H.R.	L. Sto.	Odin	
Webster G.W.	Era. 3	Thorn	
Weeden W.H.	Sto. 1	Porpoise	
Weeks C.H.	A.B.	Thames	
Weeks H.H.	S. Lt. RNR	P.615	
Weetman A.	L. Sto.	Tetrarch	
Weir J.C.	L. Tel.	Parthian	
Welburn T.H.	Sto. 1	Grampus	
Welfoot C.C.	P.O.	Untamed	
Welham F.	A.B.	Umpire	
Wells G.H.	Sto. 1	Narwhal	
Wells L.H.	A.B.	Tigris	
Welshman M.W.	C.P.O.	Stratagem	
Wentworth S.	A.B.	Regent	
Wescott J.E.	L. Sto.	Regulus	
Wesson R.R.	A.B.	Seahorse	
West E.F.	L. Sto.	H.49	
West K.J.	Tel.	Utmost	
West K.R.	P.O. Tel.	Utmost	
West P.	L. Sea.	Pandora	
Westbrook C.T.	L. Tel.	Triad	
Westbury E.G.	A.B.	Seahorse	
Westbury J.	Sto. 1	Triton	
Weston J.	Sto. 1	Porpoise	
Westwood A.L.	A.B.	Stratagem	
Whalebone F.J.	C.P.O.	Narwhal	
Whalley J.	Elec. Art. 2	Perseus	
Wheble R. de la F.	Elec. Art. 3	Parthian	
Wheeler F.	A.B.	Thistle	
Wheeler F.E.T.	Sto. 1	Sterlet	
Wheeler F.T.	L. Sto.	Turbulent	
Wheeler J.W.	Sto. P.O.	Talisman	
Wheeler R.	A.B.	Untamed	
Wheldon H.W.	A.B.	Turbulent	
Whincup A.L.	L. Sto.	Parthian	
Whitbread H.J.W.	P.O.	Thunderbolt	DSM
White A.C.	A.B.	Utmost	
White C.H.	P.O.	Triad	DSM

White C.W.	A.B.	H.49	
White D.H.	A.B.	Thunderbolt	
White D.P.	A.B.	Odin	
White D.W.	L. Sea.	Olympus	
White G.F.	P.O.	Regulus	
White G.H.	A.B.	Usurper	
White J.	A.B.	Rainbow	
White J.H.	P.O.	Seahorse	
White K.R.	Sto. 1	Snapper	
White P.J.	A.B.	Snapper	
White R.A.	P.O.	Olympus	
White S.R.	Lt. Cmdr.	Narwhal	
White W.J.	Tel.	Triumph	DSM*
White W.P.	Era. 4	Urge	
Whitebread A.E.	L. Sto.	Triad	
Whitehead C.C.	L. Sea.	Tetrarch	
Whiteway- Wilkinson R.D.	Lt.	P.33	DSC
Whitfield H.C.	A.B.	Tempest	
Whitfield L.G.H.	Sto. 1	Usurper	
Whiting J.B.	Sto. P.O.	Trooper	
Whittaker E.	L. Sig.	Salmon	DSM
Whittaker J.	Sto. 1	Thistle	
Whittaker R.	A.B.	Porpoise	
Whittle J.	L. Sto.	Grampus	
Whyte A.M.	Era. 4	Perseus	
Whyte H. McL.	Era. 4	Turbulent	
Whyte J.	Sto. 1	Regulus	
Wickenden C.A.B.	P.O.	Traveller	
Wickham W.L.J.	Sto. P.O.	Triumph	
Wickstead E.J.	Sto. 1	Union	
Wilby K.G.	Sto. 1	Utmost	
Wilcock T.	A.B.	P.222	
Wild J.R.	Lt. RNR	Traveller	
Wild S.M.	Era. 3	Taciturn	
Wildman R.	A.B.	Urge	
Wiles M.C.W.	A.B.	Tigris	
Wilford J.F.	S. Lt. RNVR	Olympus	
Wilkes G.H.	C.P.O.	Turbulent	DSM
Wilkes S.C.	L. Sto.	Urge	
Wilkins J.T.H.	A.B.	Rainbow	
Wilkinson A.T.	Wrnt. Engr.	Orpheus	
Wilkinson F.	Era. 2	Triumph	
Wilkinson J.T.	Sto. 1	Triton	
Wilkinson L.	Elec. Art. 1	P.222	
Wilkinson W.L.	A.B.	Regulus	
Wilks W.H.	Tel.	Regent	
Willcocks A.C.	Era. 4	Syrtis	
Willcocks H.A.	Sto. 1	Sickle	
Willcocks R.B.	Ord. Sea.	Tetrarch	
Willcox E.G.	L. Sea.	Grampus	
Williams A.F.C.	P.O.	Porpoise	
Williams A.V.	Tel.	Utmost	
Williams B.	Sto. P.O.	Union	
Williams C.	Sto. 1	Phoenix	
Williams C.	Sto. 1	Porpoise	
Williams C.D.	A.B.	P.48	
Williams D.	L. Sea.	Utmost	
Williams D.I.	A.B.	Tempest	
Williams F.J.	Tel.	Spearfish	
Williams G.A.	A.B.	Turbulent	
Williams H.C.	Tel.	Swordfish	
Williams H.V.	Era. 3	Thule	
Williams I.G.	A.B.	Usk	
Williams L.	L. Sea.	Trooper	
Williams L.P.	L. Sea.	Salmon	
Williams R.G.	Era. 4	Stratagem	
Williams R.H.	A.B.	Swordfish	
Williams W.	A.B.	Vandal	
Williams W.R.	Tel.	Triad	MID
Willicombe T.J.	Sto. 1	Turbulent	
Willmott M.	Lt. Cmdr.	Talisman	
Wilson A.N.	Ch. Era.	Narwhal	
Wilson C.	Era. 4	Tetrarch	
Wilson C.C.	S. Lt. RNR	Grampus	
Wilson D.R.	A.B.	P.514	
Wilson E.	A.B.	Odin	
Wilson E.E.G.	Sto. 1	Triumph	DSM
Wilson F.G.	L. Ck.	Olympus	
Wilson H.	A.B.	Unsparing	
Wilson H.D.	A.B.	Thunderbolt	
Wilson H.R.	L. Sea.	Oxley	
Wilson J.R.	L. Sea.	Parthian	
Wilson L.E.	A.B.	Syrtis	
Wilson R.	A.B.	Triumph	
Wilson R.A.	P.O. Ck. (s)	Traveller	
Wilson R.D.	Era. 4	Utmost	DSM
Wilson W.	P.O.	Simoon	
Wiltshire M.R.	Sto. 1	Phoenix	
Wimble W.	Sto. 1	Porpoise	
Winder A.R.	P.O.	Rover	
Winder J.T.	Era. 4	Snapper	
Windham J.O.	Era. 2	P.222	
Windley H.S.	A.B.	Seahorse	
Wingrave G.C.	L. Sea.	Phoenix	
Wingrove R.H.	A.B.	Thorough	
Winter A.L.	Era. 4	Virtue	
Winter J.	A.B.	P.32	
Winter J.L.	A.B.	Tempest	
Winter R.H.	L. Sto.	Tetrarch	
Winterbottom F.W.L.	Lt.	Stratagem	
Wisdom R.E.	A.B.	Usurper	
Wise J.A.S.	Lt. Cmdr.	Orpheus	
Wiseman P.D.	P.O. Tel.	Urge	MID
Wishart R.W.	L. Sto.	Untamed	
Witham L.R.	Sto. 1	Talisman	
Withey W.R.	Lt. (E)	Rainbow	
Wolfe G.A.	Era. 4	Parthian	
Wolverson J.T.	P.O. Tel.	P.33	DSM
Wood A.J.	P.O. Ck. (s)	Narwhal	
Wood B.J.	Sto. 1	Thorn	
Wood D.J.	Sto. 1	Vandal	
Wood E.A.	Ch. Era.	Thorn	
Wood F.H.	L. Sea.	Orpheus	
Wood G.	Era.	Talisman	
Wood H.M.S.	L. Sig.	Triad	
Wood J.C.H.	S. Lt. RNR	Utmost	
Wood J.H.	Tel.	Swordfish	
Wood R.	L. Sto.	Sterlet	
Wood T.D.	Sto. 1	Narwhal	
Wood W.	Tel.	Stonehenge	
Woodards F.C.	Sto. 1	Syrtis	
Woodcock D.A.M.	Wrnt. Engr.	Thunderbolt	
Woodcock F.H.	L. Sea.	Utmost	
Woodcock G.H.	A.B.	Rainbow	
Woodfield L.N.	L. Stwd.	Oswald	
Woodhead A.	Era. 3	Rainbow	
Woodman E.J.H.	A.B.	Unique	

oods B.C.	A.B.	Regent	
oods K. Mac I.	Lt. Cmdr.	Odin	
oodward L.	L. Sea.	Oxley	
oodward S.	L. Sto.	Porpoise	
oolley J.E.	L. Tel.	Stratagem	
oollatt A.A.	Sto. P.O.	Sickle	
oolrich J.E.	L. Sto.	Urge	
orland A.G.	Ord. Sea.	Unique	
orlock W.H.G.	A.B.	P.514	
orral J.E.W.	Act. S. Lt. RNR	Thames	
orrall H.T.	A.B.	Undaunted	
orth A.G.	A.B.	Tempest	
orth D.T.	L. Sea.	Pandora	
orth J.H.	Lt.	Usurper	
orth W.N.	Era. 3	Oxley	
orthington F.	Sto. 1	Parthian	
otherspoon J.W.J.	Era. 1	Perseus	
ren C.B.L.	Lt. Cmdr. RNR	Tarpon	
rennall H.	L. Sto.	Rainbow	
right A.A.	L. Sto.	Rainbow	
right G.H.A.	Sto. P.O.	Unbeaten	DSM
right G.J.	Lt.	Sterlet	
right G.M.D.	Lt. (E)	Triumph	MBE DSC
right J.	Sto. 1	Porpoise	
yatt H.	Era. 3	Triton	
ykeham-Martin M.F.	Lt.	Salmon	
tes R.M.	L. Sto.	Narwhal	
oman R.A.	P.O.	Trooper	
elding H.A.	A.B.	Sickle	
rk T.	P.O. Stwd.	Thunderbolt	
ung D.G.W.	A.B.	Undaunted	
ung F.J.	L. Sea.	Rainbow	
ung H.H.	P.O.	Unbeaten	
ung W.	Sto. 1	Syrtis	
ille J.B.	P.O. Tel.	Union	
ppi G.W.	Ch. Era.	Phoenix	

Buckingham Palace 1942
Crew of Torbay. Skipper - Commander A. Miers VC

Contents - Final Item

Miscellaneous items of submarine interest; among which are unidentified photographs needing further research.
We would welcome any information from Submariners or Royal Navy readers to enable us to finalise our archive memorabilia.

Visit to mystery small submarine? Gallipoli c.1919

New Entry May 1929

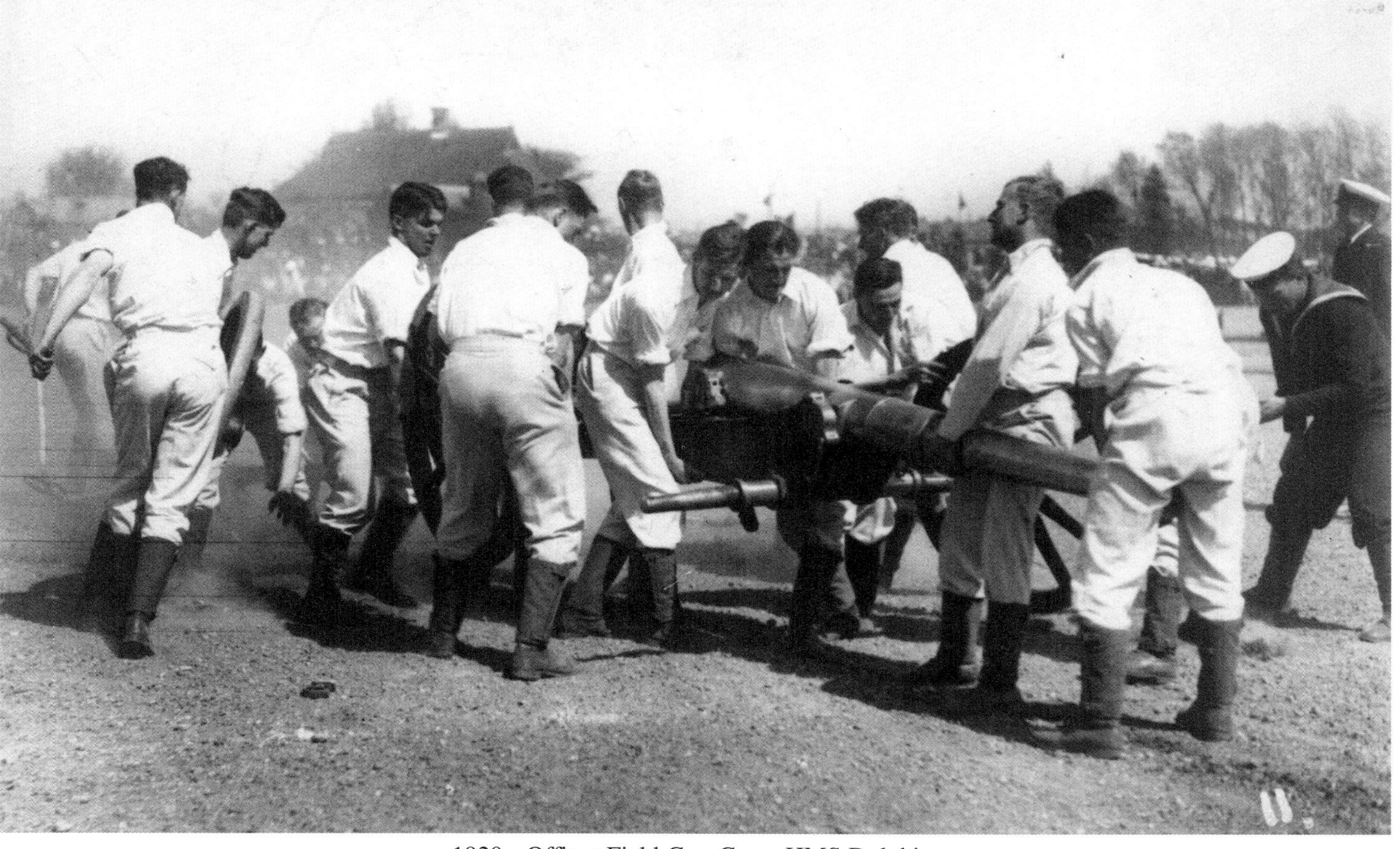

1929 - Officer Field Gun Crew, HMS Dolphin.

Budding Submariners
Donald Dunkelley, lost on 'Thames' left back row

HMS Sparrowhawk - Orkneys. Torpedo maintenance shop RN & RAF.
Dennis Peel (Gatwick Member) Left Foreground.

Japanese Submarines (Tokyo?) Believed to be British 'C' Class Boats; Japan had an alliance with the UK during the First World War.

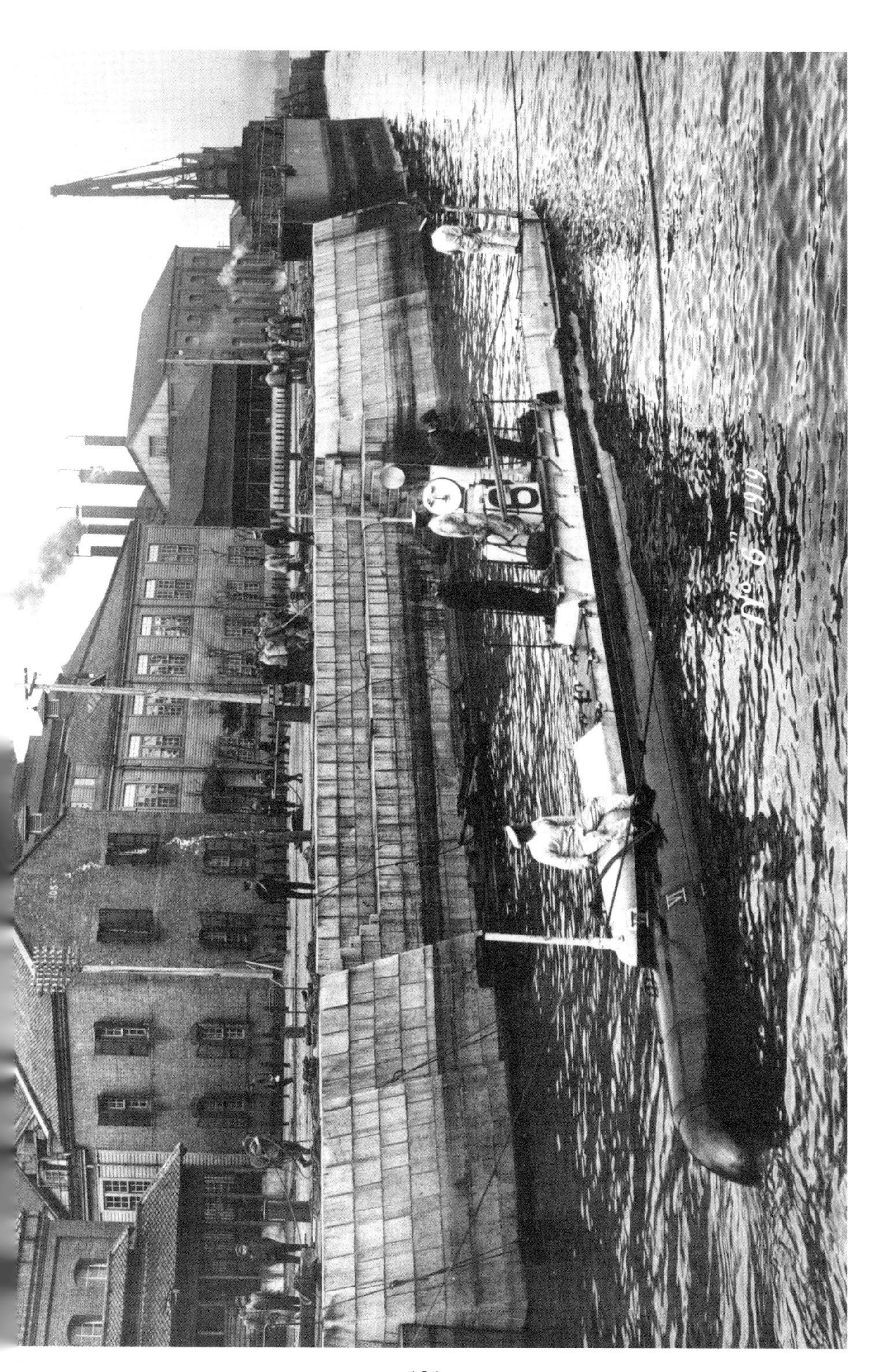

Crossing the Atlantic

Crossing the line. Clyde 1930s

Keith Nethercoate-Bryant & George Tranter
HMS/M Artemis 1940s

British Submarines 'Frozen in time' Gulf of Finland World War I
An earlier 'Cold War' scene

Anzac Submariners

Control Panel and Fessenden Equipment L3?

Hydroplane Operators Position L3?

Motor Room Switchgear L3?

Torpedo Tubes Believed to be L3

P 355 T-Class Submarine Thermopylae

List of Casualties from HMS/M Thetis Following Sea Trials Accident June 1st 1939

Surname	Rank	Christian Names
Officers		
Bolus RN	Lieut/Cmdr	Guy Howard
ChapmanRN	Lieut	Harold
Poland RN	Lieut	William Anthony Weston
Glenn RN	Warrant Engineer	Roy Demetrius
Ratings		
Cornish	Chief Petty Officer	George P
Mitchell	Petty Officer	E
Goad	Petty Officer	T T
Smithers	Petty Officer	C E
Hope	Petty Officer Telegraphist	J A
Hughes	Petty Officer Cook	J C
Byrne	Electrical Artificer	A W
Ormes	Chief Engine Room Art	W C
Jackson	Chief Engine Room Art	P F
Creasy	Engine Room Artificer	J C
French	Engine Room Artificer	H W E
Howells	Engine Room Artificer	H G
Dillon-Shallard	Chief Stoker	H J
Wells	Stoker/Petty Officer	J W
Hambrook	Leading Seaman	W L
Luck	Leading Seaman	W A
Read	Leading Seaman	J A
Smith	Leading Seaman	A H
Stevens	Leading Seaman	S W G
Batten	Leading Signalman	F B
Allan	Leading Telegraphist	W E
Harward	Leading Telegraphist	K A
Stock	Leading Steward	F N
Costley	Able Seaman	J
Crombleholme	Able Seaman	S
Kendrick	Able Seaman	E A
Longstaff	Able Seaman	N
Morgans	Able Seaman	J A
Rogers	Able Seaman	F
Turner	Able Seaman	J H
Wilson	Able Seaman	T
Graham	Telegraphist	C T W
Mortimer	Telegraphist	T W
Brooke	Leading Stoker	R S
Cunningham	Leading Stoker	D

Feeney	Leading Stoker	J S
Kenney	Leading Stoker	T W
Youles	Leading Stoker	E J
Bambrick	Stoker	T
Craig	Stoker	J
Dunn	Stoker	A H
Green	Stoker	L E
Hills	Stoker	A G
Hole	Stoker	W T
Matthews	Stoker	W A
Orrock	Stoker	W
Yates	Stoker	A E

Officers of Submarine Building at Cammel Laird

Garnett RN	Lieut/Cmdr	Richard Newstead
Lloyd RN	Lieut/Cmdr	Thomas Clive Conway
Ryan RN	Lieut	Patrick Edward James
Jamison RN	Lieut (E)	Anthony Geoffrey

Other Naval Officers

Hayter RN	Cmdr	Reginald George Bazai
Pennington RN	Cmdr (E)	Lionel Grant
Jackson RN (OBE)	Engineer Captain	Stanley
Henderson RN	Lieut (E)	Colin Maxwell Hume

Admiralty & Overseeing Officers

Surname	**Job Title**	**Christian Names**
Aslett Mr	Assistant	William Henry
Bailey Mr	Constructor RCNC Admiralty	Frank
Gisborne Mr	Instructor Of Ship Wrights	Edward
Hill Mr	Principal Ship Overseer	Albert Adair Fitzgerald
Horne Mr	Asst Engineer Overseer	Charles William
Horsman Mr	Asst Ship Fitting Overseer	Harry Rushworth
Hunn Mr	Electrical Engineer Admiralty	Leslie William

Employees of Cammel Laird & Co Ltd

Armstrong Mr	Electrical Engineer Manager	J I
Crout Mr	Asst Ship Yard Manager	R W
Kipling Mr	Foreman Caulker	R
Owen Mr	Foreman Electrician	W
Robinson Mr	Foreman Engineer	A B
Rogerson Mr	Asst Engineer Manager	R
Watkinson Mr	Asst Engineer Manager	A S
Beatty Mr	Caulker	W B

Broad Mr	Electrician	S
Chinn Mr	Electrician	A G
Hamilton Mr	Electrician	C J S
Lewis Mr	Electrician	E H
Smith Mr	Electrician	W H
Somers Mr	Electrician	G A
Bresner Mr	Engine Fitter	F R
Brown Mr	Engine Fitter	W
Eccleston Mr	Engine Fitter	H
Griffiths Mr	Engine Fitter	J
Homer Mr	Engine Fitter	R
Page Mr	Engine Fitter	J A
Quinn Mr	Engine Fitter	P L
Smith Mr	Engine Fitter	C
Craven Mr	Ship Fitter	A
Scarth Mr	Ship Fitter	G L
Watterson Mr	Ship Fitter	W

Employees of Vickers Armstrong Ltd

Ankers Mr	T
Cragg Mr	H T
Tyler Mr	D V
Young Mr	J

Employees of Brown Bros & Co Ltd

Duncan Mr	D N

Mersey Pilot

Willcox Mr	N D

Employees of City Caterers (Liverpool) Ltd

Bath Mr	W G
Dobells Mr	G H